# PEACE Makers

## 13 Fun Filled Bible Lessons About Peace

### Susan L. Lingo

STANDARD PUBLISHING

Cincinnati, Ohio

# DEDICATION

**Peacemakers who sow in peace
raise a harvest of righteousness
James 3:18**

Peace Makers
© 2001 Susan L. Lingo

Published by Standard Publishing, Cincinnati, Ohio
A division of Standex International Corporation

## Credits

Produced by Susan L. Lingo, Bright Ideas Books™
Cover design by Diana Walters
Illustrated by Marilynn G. Barr and Megan E. Jeffery

08 07 06 05 04 03 02 01  5 4 3 2 1
ISBN 0-7847-1233-6
Printed in the United States of America

# CONTENTS

# INTRODUCTION

## POWERING UP YOUR KIDS' FAITH!

Congratulations! You are about to embark on a wonderful and powerful mission to strengthen, energize, and stabilize your kids' faith and fundamental knowledge of God—faith and fundamentals that will launch your kids powerfully into the twenty-first century!

*Peace Makers* is part of the Power Builders Series, an exciting and powerfully effective curriculum that includes *Faith Finders, Servant Leaders, Disciple Makers, Value Seekers, Hope Finders, Joy Builders, Power Boosters,* and the book you're now holding. *Peace Makers* is dedicated to exploring what it takes to be God's peacemakers and how we can bring peace into today's—and tomorrow's—world. Thirteen theme-oriented lessons will help your kids explore, assess, and apply God's truths that relate to peace and being peacemakers in an often unfriendly world. And woven throughout each lesson is Scripture, Scripture, and more Scripture!

Each lesson in *Peace Makers* has the following features:

**POWER FOCUS** (Approximate time: 10 minutes)—You'll begin with a mighty motivator to get kids thinking about the focus of the lesson. This may include an eye-popping devotion, a simple game, or another lively attention-getting tool. Also included are interactive discussion and a brief overview of what kids will be learning during the lesson. *Purpose: To focus attention and cue kids in to what they'll be learning during the lesson.*

**MIGHTY MESSAGE** (Approximate time: 15 minutes)—This is the body of the lesson and includes engaging Bible passages that actively teach about the lesson's theme. The Mighty Message is not just "another Bible story," so your kids will discover God's truths through powerful passages and important portions of Scripture that are supported by additional verses and made relevant to kids' lives. Processing questions help kids explore each side of the passages and their relation to the theme, beginning with easier questions for young children and ending with more challenging think-about-it questions for older kids. Meaty and memorable, this lesson section will help kids learn tremendous truths! *Purpose: To teach powerful biblical truths and offer thought-provoking discussion in age-appropriate ways.*

**MESSAGE IN MOTION** (Approximate time: 10-15 minutes)—This section contains engaging activities that enrich and reinforce the lesson theme. It may include creative crafts, lively games and relays, action songs and rhythmic raps, mini service projects, and much more. *Purpose: To enrich learning in memorable and fun ways that build a sense of community.*

**SUPER SCRIPTURE** (Approximate time: 10-15 minutes)—This all-important section encourages and helps kids effectively learn, understand, and apply God's Word in their lives. The Mighty Memory Verse was chosen so every child can effectively learn it during the course of three weeks, but an extra-challenge verse is offered for older kids or children who can handle learning more verses. You are free to substitute your own choice of verses in this section, but please keep in mind that the activities, songs, crafts, and mnemonic devices are designed for the Mighty Memory Verse and the accompanying extra-challenge verse. And remember, when it comes to learning God's Word, effective learning takes place when kids work on only one or two verses over the course of several weeks! *Purpose: To memorize, learn, recall, and use God's Word.*

**POWERFUL PROMISE** (Approximate time: 5-10 minutes)—The lesson closes with a summary, a promise, and a prayer. You'll summarize the lesson, the Mighty Memory Verse, and the theme, then challenge kids to make a special commitment to God for the coming week. The commitments are theme-related and give kids a chance to put their faith into action. Finally, a brief prayer and responsive farewell blessing end the lesson. *Purpose: To make a commitment of faith to God and express thanks and praise to him.*

**POWER PAGE!** (Take-home paper)—Each lesson ends with a fun-to-do take-along page that encourages kids to keep the learning going at home. Scripture puzzles, crafts, recipes, games, Bible read-about-its, Mighty Memory Verse reinforcement, and more challenge kids through independent discovery and learning fun. *Purpose: To reinforce, review, and enrich the day's lesson and the Mighty Memory Verse.*

**PLUS, in every Power Builder's book you'll discover these great features!**

★ **WHIZ QUIZZES!** At the end of each section is a reproducible Whiz Quiz to gently, yet effectively, assess what has been learned. Completed by kids in about five minutes at the end of lessons 3, 6, 9, and 12, the Whiz Quiz is a nonthreatening and fun measuring tool to allow teachers, kids, and parents to actually see what has been learned in the prior weeks. When kids complete each Whiz Quiz, consider presenting them a collectible surprise such as measuring cups that represent how they measure up as God's peacemakers. For example, after the first Whiz Quiz, present each child with a ¼-cup measuring cup. After the next Whiz Quiz, present ⅓-cup measuring cups. Then use ½- and 1-cup measuring cups for lessons 9 and 12. When the book is complete, kids will have a whole set of measuring cups on which they can write "Measuring up as peacemakers!" (one word on each cup). Kids will love the cool reminders of the lessons and their accomplishments! Be sure to keep children's completed Whiz Quiz pages in folders to present to kids at the end of the book or at the end of the year, in combination with other Whiz Quizzes from different books in the Power Builders Series.

★ **LESSON 13 REVIEW!** The last lesson in *Peace Makers* is an important review of all that's been learned, applied, accomplished, and achieved during the past twelve weeks. Kids will love the lively review games, action songs, unique review tools, and celebratory feel of this special lesson!

★ **SCRIPTURE STRIPS!** At the back of the book, you'll discover every Mighty Memory Verse and extra-challenge verse that appears in *Peace Makers*. These reproducible Scripture strips can be copied and cut apart to use over and over for crafts, games, cards, bookmarks, and other fun and fabulous "you-name-its"! Try gluing these strips to long Formica chips to make colorful, clattery key chains that double as super Scripture reviews!

★ **TEACHER FEATURE!** Discover timeless teaching tips and hints, hands-on help, and a whole lot more in this mini teacher workshop. Every book in the Power Builders series offers a unique Teacher Feature that helps leaders understand and teach through issues such as discipline, prayer, Scripture memory, and more. The Teacher Feature in *Peace Makers* is "Creating an Atmosphere for Learning."

God bless you as you teach with patience, love, and this powerful resource to help launch kids into another century of love, learning, and serving God! More POWER to you!

# CREATING AN ATMOSPHERE FOR LEARNING

Do you have a fear of elevators or closed-in spaces? If you answered yes, chances are you had a negative experience in the place you now steer fervently clear of. A learned response to a particular place can be unnervingly negative or pleasantly positive. It's the same with classroom learning. Most teachers spend a great deal of time and effort planning what will be learned and how to present it but often give little consideration to *where* learning takes place. Creating an atmosphere for learning can be the deciding factor in whether kids will learn smoothly and memorably or carry little home in their hearts. Let's take a brief look at how to create an atmosphere that makes the most of classroom space and style as it strengthens the effectiveness of lessons.

**Creating an *emotional* atmosphere.** An atmosphere for well-being is vitally important for effective learning and in itself can impart Christian values you desire your kids to nurture. Best of all, creating an atmosphere of well-being isn't as tough as it sounds! Warmly welcome kids each time they come to class. Repeating a child's name and giving a pat on the shoulder or a quick hug tells a child, "I'm happy to see you. You matter to me!" Be careful not to condescend to kids by expecting too little of them or by speaking in language that is too young, especially for third through sixth graders. Accept that kids can take responsibility in helping around the classroom and even in presenting some of the prayers, devotions, Bible stories, or games. Letting kids know you trust them and expect them to achieve helps motivate learning. Kids pick up quickly on your levels of respect and expectations and thrive on the challenges and stimulation you encourage. And don't forget Ephesians 4:32: "Be kind and compassionate to one another, forgiving each other, just as in Christ God forgave you." This verse offers great advice for kids and teachers alike and will help create an atmosphere where everyone feels valued, accepted, respected, and welcomed!

**Creating a *physical* atmosphere.** Setting up your room for the most effective use of space while at the same time giving it an air of excitement can be challenging—especially if you're borrowing temporary space from a school or other classroom. After all, *how* can you just up and move entire bulletin boards and other displays? Actually, it's not as hard as it seems. Portable bulletin boards can be made from a variety of materials, including cork stapled to plywood, acoustic ceiling squares, or even large boxes that offer awesome 3-D views! Simply add your chosen background materials, title, and illustrations or displays for portable, colorful bulletin boards. Whether you're in a makeshift classroom or your own permanent area, be sure to change your displays each month and to look for ways to exhibit kids' work, Scripture reminders, and displays kids help create.

Seating in classrooms can be strategic and allow you to help kids who may be distracted easily or yearn for attention. Place tables or chairs in a U-shape where everyone's view is toward the same direction. Seat no more than four kids to a table or chair-grouping, and be cagey with how you let kids arrange themselves. If you have one or two very active kids, place them in groups with quieter children. Seat kids with ADHD close to where you might be standing or sitting to help them focus better. Finally, change seating regularly to give kids a chance to form relationships with others.

Creating a bit of personal space in classrooms is important, and kids love their own little spaces, nooks, and niches. Use large golf umbrellas to make cozy nooks for reading Bible stories or working on memory verses. Turn tables on their sides to give small groups their own places to practice skits or puppet shows. Hang festive fabric awnings in corners or drape fabric over tables for more quiet places to pray, praise, or play quiet learning games. Awarding time in these nifty nooks is a great way to encourage kids to get their work done or to keep focused during lessons.

Finally, quick classroom props can add delightful touches that make Bible stories and lessons even more memorable. Drape solid-colored fabric over tall tomato cages and let kids use fabric paint to make adorable Bible characters. Add tactile touches such as fiberfill for beards and hair and rope for belts and headdresses. Make an oasis by covering large, sturdy mailing tubes with crinkled grocery sacks and adding large green construction-paper fronds. Scatter the trees around the room or cut the tubes in half to place against walls. (Tape the trunks to the walls to keep them firmly planted!)

**Creating a *spiritual* atmosphere.** Creating a spiritual atmosphere involves making your classroom a place in which Christian values are regarded, respected, and even celebrated! Instead of traditional "rules for the classroom," post a series of five paraphrased Scripture verses that exemplify the values you want your kids to cherish. For example, consider using the sample classroom code in the box below. (If you want, simply photocopy and enlarge the box to use right away!)

Nurture a spirit of acceptance for others and be inclusive in games, parties, picnics, and all class functions. Kids yearn to be a part of a group and need to know they're accepted for who they are—not who you wish they'd be! Finally, be gracious about thanking kids and letting them know they are precious to you and even more precious to God! Little notes and cards don't spoil kids—they lift them spiritually!

Creating an atmosphere for learning is fun and functional for you, and it can be exciting and inviting for kids. Be creative, think out of the box, turn innovative, and be delighted as you discover ways to create an atmosphere in your classroom that's as special as you and your kids are in God's eyes!

# CLASSROOM CODE

1. *Treat others as you would like to be treated. (Matthew 7:12)*
2. *Be a peacemaker, and God will be pleased! (Matthew 5:9)*
3. *Forgive others as Jesus has forgiven you. (Ephesians 4:32)*
4. *Serve each other in love and kindness. (Galatians 5:13)*
5. *In all things, be thankful! (1 Thessa-lonians 5:18)*

# PARENT PAGE NEWSLETTER

Dear Parent:

Your child is about to embark on a wonderful exploration of peace and what it means to be God's Peacemaker! In the book *Peace Makers,* children will discover the three all-powerful sources of our peace, how obeying God brings serenity, that Jesus died for our sins so we could live at peace with God, how being led by the Holy Spirit brings order and empowerment to our lives, how we can be at peace with family and friends, what "world peace" really means, plus much more. You can help in your child's learning process by:

★ joining in the fun of the take-home Power Pages,

★ discussing with your child peaceful solutions to family problems,

★ helping your child learn the Mighty Memory Verses,

★ reading Bible verses on peace and being peacemakers,

★ portraying a positive role-model for peace and patience, and

★ inquiring how your child is doing on the Whiz Quiz reviews.

Being a part of your child's growing spiritual experience brings wonderful opportunities to share your own faith and love for God. God bless you as you discover God's perfect peace and purpose in being his Peacemakers!

*Let the peace of Christ rule in your hearts, since as members of one body you were called to peace. And be thankful.*
*Colossians 3:15*

# AT PEACE WITH OUR GOD

Submit to God and be
at peace with him;
in this way prosperity
will come to you.
Job 22:21

# THE WAY TO OBEY

Obeying God brings peace and prosperity.

Job 22:21
Psalms 4:8; 29:11
1 Corinthians 14:33
James 4:7

## SESSION SUPPLIES

★ Bibles
★ unsalted crackers
★ markers
★ scissors & tape
★ plastic knives & napkins
★ peanut butter
★ a paper sack
★ newsprint
★ salt
★ construction paper
★ small, disposable salt shakers (one per child)
★ photocopies of Job 22:21 (page 127)
★ photocopies of the Power Page! (page 19)

## MIGHTY MEMORY VERSE

Submit to God and be at peace with him; in this way prosperity will come to you. Job 22:21

## SESSION OBJECTIVES

During this session, children will
★ discover that obedience and peace are related
★ understand there is no peace without obeying God
★ explore what God's peace brings
★ learn how our attitudes affect obedience

## BIBLE BACKGROUND

You've undoubtedly heard it said that there's no rest for the weary. But perhaps an even more striking and important truth is that *there's no peace without obedience!* God's peace is consuming and powerful, and it is there for us in even the most disturbing moments of our lives when every act or word seems out of control. But like other responsibilities in lives centered around God, it's up to us to take that first step and choose obedience to God. Obedience to God with a willing spirit and cheerful heart is the key to receiving God's peace and serenity that quiets even the most distressed, disorganized, and disturbed of lives.

Kids feel frazzled every bit as much as adults in today's hustle-bustle world. They crave the peace and calm that only God can provide. But kids need to understand that God's peace is a result of their own choices in obeying our heavenly Father and not in the false pacification or appeasement found in outside influences such as money, movies, or music. Use this lesson to help kids discover that true peace begins with their willing obedience to God and his will.

# POWER FOCUS

Before class, write the following directions on slips of paper, one step per slip.

*Step 1. Place a napkin in front of you.*

*Step 2. Get a cracker.*

*Step 3. Pick up a plastic knife.*

*Step 4. Spread on the peanut butter.*

*Step 5. Put a cracker on top.*

Place the directions in a paper sack and scramble them up. Set peanut butter, crackers, napkins, and plastic knives on a table.

Welcome kids, then invite them to form pairs or trios and gather around the table. Say: **Let's try a little experiment. I have the directions for making a snack in this paper bag, but the directions are a bit mixed up. We'll pull the directions out one at a time and do exactly what they tell us. Then we'll see what kind of snacks we end up with!**

Have kids take turns pulling out directions, reading them aloud, and following them exactly. Be prepared—you may end up with some crazy snack results! When you've followed every direction, say: **Wow! I guess our snacks didn't turn out as we might have hoped, did they? What do you think might happen if we follow each direction carefully and in order? Let's find out.**

Repeat the snack preparations, but read the steps in order. When you're done, you'll have yummy peanut-butter-and-cracker sandwiches. As kids nibble their snacks, ask:

★ **Why did our snacks turn out good the second time?**

★ **How did carefully following the directions help?**

★ **In what ways is this like following God's directions carefully?**

★ **What happens when we disobey God? when we obey him?**

Say: **Making these snacks reminds us about obeying God's commands and his wise directions for our lives. When we disobey God, things don't work out smoothly and peacefully. But when we follow God and obey him, our lives become filled with peace, love, happiness, and**

**other wonderful blessings.** Read aloud Job 22:21, then say: **When we submit to God and obey him, we have powerful peace in our lives. For the next several weeks we'll be learning a lot about peace. We'll explore where our peace comes from and how we can be peacemakers that God smiles upon!**

**Today we'll be learning how peace is a gift that comes from obeying God and that God's peace fills our lives with wonderful blessings. Right now, let's explore the peace that comes from obeying God with all our hearts, minds, and souls.**

## THE **MIGHTY** MESSAGE

Have kids form four groups and give every group a piece of newsprint and a marker. Assign each group one of the following Scripture references to look up, then have kids jot down what God gives us through his peace: Job 22:21 (prosperity); Psalm 4:8 (sleep and safety); Psalm 29:11 (strength and blessings); and James 4:7 (power to resist Satan and evils). After a minute or so, have each group read aloud its verse and tell what God gives us through his peace. Ask:

★ **Why does obeying God bring us peace and prosperity?**

★ **In what ways can we obey God?**

★ **How does having God's peace help us serve him? serve others? follow God more closely?**

Say: **When we submit to God and obey him, God gives us wonderful peace, which in turn brings us prosperity, peaceful sleep, safety and strength, resistance to Satan, and much more. Ahh, what glorious peace comes from obeying God! But did you know that just obeying isn't enough? Let's nibble another cracker to see what else needs to be present when we obey.**

Distribute unsalted crackers and have kids take a bite. Say: **These crackers taste kind of flat and dull, don't they? That's because they're missing the salt to spice them up. Here—try a bit of salt with your next bite.** Sprinkle a bit of salt on each cracker. Then say: **Crackers without salt are okay to eat, but they are even better with a bit of salt to add spice. That's how it**

**POWER POINTERS**

Help kids understand that "submission" is an attitude whereby we surrender our self-centered wills and that "obedience" is the act of obeying. With God, we want to do both!

is when we obey God. It's not enough simply to obey; it's the heart with which we obey that really counts! The Bible tells us not just to serve others but to serve in *love.* We're to give to others, but to give with *cheerful* hearts. In the same way, we're not simply to obey in a begrudging or cranky way but rather by salting our obedience with willing attitudes and cheerful hearts. Listen to what the Bible says about having salt in our lives.

Read aloud Mark 9:50, then say: **Having salt in our lives means adding the spice that makes our attitudes sweet and "tasty" to God, such as willingness, love, and cheer. If we lose that saltiness, it's very hard to get it back. God wants us to have good atti-tudes about obeying so we may be at peace with him and others.** Ask:

★ **In what ways do our attitudes affect our obedience toward God?**

★ **How can having a cheerful, willing attitude bring peace to our lives?**

Say: **Our attitudes are key when it comes to obeying God, and we've learned today that without obeying God there is no peace. In Isaiah 48:22, God himself says, "There is no peace for the wicked." That truth is very important to remember! Now let's make cool salt shakers to remind us of the importance of obeying God with willingness and cheerfulness so we can be at peace.**

## THE MESSAGE IN MOTION

Before class, purchase a disposable salt shaker (filled with salt) for each child. These nifty, inexpensive shakers are available where you find picnic supplies. Cut strips of white construction paper to fit over the labels of the salt shakers. Kids will be decorating these new labels.

Invite kids to work in pairs and hand everyone a salt shaker. Explain that kids will be making new labels to put on their salt shakers so they can be placed on dinner tables to share with families as reminders of obeying God and being at peace. Have kids write Mark 9:50b on their shakers: "Have salt in your-selves, and be at peace with each other." Tape the labels around the salt shakers, then invite kids to decorate the labels with colorful designs such as hearts, stars, or fancy squiggles. As kids work, remind them that there is no peace without obeying God and that God's peace brings us many blessings.

When the salt shakers are finished, say: **This Scripture verse reminds us to be at peace with others, and that includes the people in our families. Each time you or someone in your family uses your salt shaker, remember that peace begins with obeying God and that our obedience must be salted with willing submission and cheerful hearts. Now let's begin to learn an important Scripture verse about submitting to God and being at peace with him.**

## SUPER SCRIPTURE

Before class, photocopy the Scripture strip for Job 22:21 (page 127), one for each child, and cut out the strips. Then write the Mighty Memory Verse on newsprint as follows:

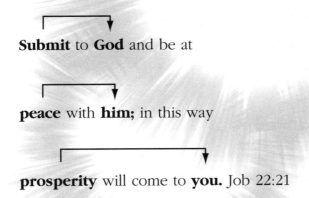

**Submit** to **God** and be at

**peace** with **him;** in this way

**prosperity** will come to **you.** Job 22:21

Be sure that the words "Submit," "peace," and "prosperity" are aligned on the left in dark print and that arrows are drawn to "God," "him," and "you" respectively. Tape the verse to the wall or a door so kids can see and read it.

Gather kids by the Mighty Memory Verse and say: **Our Mighty Memory Verse this month is one of my favorites because it contains a promise. The verse is Job 22:21. Can you find it in your Bibles?** Allow time for kids to locate the verse and invite several volunteers to read the verse aloud.

Say: **I have Job 22:21 written on this paper, and I've drawn arrows to help you remember the verse. The Mighty Memory Verse says that if we do two things, God will do something for us. If we "submit to God" and** "be at peace with him," then God will prosper us or bring prosperity. *Prosperity* means "abundance," "well-being," or "showered with God's blessings"!

**I have red and yellow markers here. Who can find what we're to do in this verse? We'll make those arrows red.** Have two kids locate the arrows connecting "submit to God" and "peace with him" and trace the arrows red to symbolize obeying God with our hearts. Then have kids find the portion of the verse that tells what God will do for us ("prosperity will come to you") and trace that arrow yellow to symbolize God's rich blessings.

Repeat the verse aloud three more times, then say: **This is a great verse to remember because it tells us where peace begins—it begins with obeying God. Let's ask for God's help in having willing, obedient hearts that can receive the peace God offers us.** Hand kids the Scripture strips to take home to work on during the week. Save the newsprint with the Mighty Memory Verse to use next week.

## A POWERFUL PROMISE

Have kids sit in a circle and observe a few moments of silence. Then quietly say: **Peace and the wonderful, serene feeling that comes with peace feel good, don't they? We've learned today that we receive peace from God. We've also discovered that obeying God is the beginning of peace and that without obedience to God there is no peace. We've learned that God's peace brings blessings, safety, prosperity, and resistance to evil. And we have explored how a willing attitude and cheerful heart help us obey God even better. We also began learning a Mighty Memory Verse, which says** (encourage kids to repeat the verse with you), **"Submit to God and be at peace with him; in this way prosperity will come to you" Job 22:21.**

Hold up the Bible and read aloud 1 Corinthians 14:33. Then say: **God is a God of peace. He wants to give us peace and to prosper us, but we have to do our part. We have to obey God with** willing spirits and cheerful hearts. As we pass the Bible around the circle, you can say, "Dear Lord, please help me obey you with a cheerful, willing heart."

When everyone has held the Bible and had a chance to repeat the prayer, end with a corporate "amen." Then say: **As you leave today, remember to take along your salt shakers to remind you and your families of God's peace when we obey him in willingness and love.**

End with this responsive good-bye:

Leader: **May the God of love and peace be with you.**

Children: **And also with you!**

Distribute the Power Page! take-home papers as kids are leaving. Thank children for coming and encourage them to look for ways to obey God this week as they seek his loving peace.

# POWER PAGE!

## Who Submitted?

*Read the verses, then draw matching lines to show who submitted and how that person submitted.*

| Gen. 6:14, 22 | Joshua | went to Nineveh |
| Jonah 3:3 | David | built an ark |
| 2 Sam. 5:25 | Noah | defeated Philistines |
| Josh. 10:40 | Jonah | defeated God's enemies |

## MISSING VOWELS

*Use the letters a, e, i, o, and u to complete the Mighty Memory Verse.*

S_bm_t t_ G_d _nd b_ _t p_ _c_ w_th h_m; _n th_s w_y pr_sp_r_ty w_ll c_m_ t_ y_ _.

J_b 22:11

## Sweet Submission ... Perfect Peace!

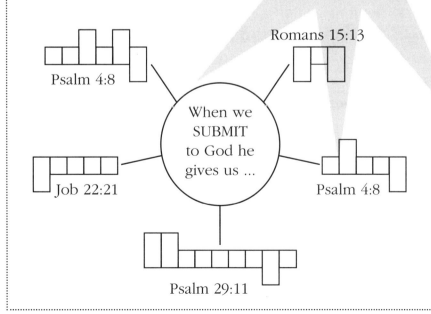

Romans 15:13

Psalm 4:8

When we SUBMIT to God he gives us ...

Job 22:21

Psalm 4:8

Psalm 29:11

### Word Bank

*blessings*

*joy*

*peace*

*safety*

*sleep*

**19**

# JESUS' PERFECT PEACE!

Peace came through Jesus' sacrifice on the cross.

Isaiah 48:18
John 14:27
Ephesians 2:13, 14, 17
Colossians 1:19, 20; 3:15

## SESSION SUPPLIES

★ Bibles
★ balloons
★ fine-tipped permanent markers
★ tape & masking tape
★ outdoor or travel magazines
★ cardboard, poster board, or foam board
★ photocopies of the Peace poem (page 26)
★ photocopies of the Power Page! (page 27)

## MIGHTY MEMORY VERSE

Submit to God and be at peace with him; in this way prosperity will come to you. Job 22:21
*(For older kids who need an extra challenge, add in Isaiah 48:22: "'There is no peace,' says the LORD, 'for the wicked.'")*

## SESSION OBJECTIVES

During this session, children will
★ realize that Jesus was God's plan for peace
★ understand that Jesus' death and resurrection bring us peace
★ explore how hope, joy, and peace are related
★ learn that nothing can take away our peace in Christ

## BIBLE BACKGROUND

Where do *you* find peace? Is it in curling up with a good book? Perhaps it's sitting beside a mountain stream or contemplating clouds on an autumn afternoon. If we think of peace and where we seek its serenity, we might be surprised to discover that those places are most often outside influences and not the peace we find in our hearts and souls from Jesus! The peace that comes through Jesus is the peace that passes all understanding and lasts forever—peace we can discover in the midst of the most crowded shopping mall or even in the center of a grieving heart.

Kids, as often as adults, search for peace outside themselves. They need to understand that the only lasting serenity comes from the peace Jesus himself presented to us when he said, "Peace I leave with you; my peace I give you" (John 14:27). Use this lesson to help kids realize the joyous truth that Jesus' own peace is given to us to rule in our hearts and direct our lives.

## POWER Focus

Place an uninflated balloon for each child at one end of the room, and have kids form three or four lines at the opposite end. Explain to kids that in this lively relay the first players in each line will hop to the balloons, inflate one and tie it off, then place the balloons between their knees and hop back to their lines so the next players can go. Continue until all the balloons are inflated and all the kids are back with their groups. Then ask:

★ **Are balloons very useable or fun before they're inflated? Explain.**

★ **How did you make these balloons useable?**

★ **How did the balloons, once they were changed, help you reach your goal?**

Say: **This relay race reminds us that not everything is useable before it's changed into something of value. Just as you transferred your air into the balloons to make them useable, Jesus transfers his love and peace to us so we can be used by God. Peace that flows from Jesus into us when we know, love, and follow him is peace that allows us to be used by God in many ways, including serving others, drawing closer to God, and being peacemakers.**

**Today we'll learn about the peace that comes from Jesus and how his sacrifice on the cross brings hope, peace, and joy into our lives. We'll discover that Christ's perfect peace within us can never be taken away. And we'll work on our Mighty Memory Verse as we explore more about the heavenly peace we receive from God and Jesus.**

But first, let's explore the peace that flows from Jesus into our hearts and how that peace changes and empowers our lives. Hold on to your balloons, because you'll need them in this next activity.

## THE MIGHTY MESSAGE

In this activity, kids will be taping their balloons to the wall or a door in the shape of a colorful, 3-D cross. You may wish to make a masking-tape outline for kids to follow when adding their balloons. Have kids sit in three groups holding their balloons. Say: **Long before Jesus was born, God was making plans for our peace. God knew that his plan was perfect and that his purpose would be fulfilled by sending Jesus to bring us peace. Let's look at God's plan, his purpose, and the presents we receive through Christ. We'll begin with God's plan for peace.** Invite two volunteers to read aloud Isaiah 48:18, 22 and 1 John 4:9. Ask:

★ **Why did God send Jesus to us?**

★ **How could Jesus bring us peace?**

Say: **God knew we were sinful and that there is no peace for the wicked. God knew we needed help! So he sent Jesus to love us, forgive us, and bring us peace. Let's have one group tape your balloons in a line across the wall to represent God's plan for our peace.** Tape the balloons close together in one or two rows (about six balloons per row) to make the cross-piece of the cross.

Say: **Now we'll read about how Jesus brought peace through his sacrifice on the cross.** Ask two volunteers to read aloud Ephesians 2:13, 14, 17 and Colossians 1:19, 20. Ask:

★ **How did Jesus dying for our sins bring us peace?**

★ **In what ways does Jesus' resurrection and triumph over death bring peace and hope?**

Say: **God's purpose in having Jesus die on the cross for our sins was to show us the way to forgiveness. Through Jesus' death and resurrection, our sins have been paid for so we can find peace in knowing we can be close to God. We also have the hope of eternal life, and that gives us peace and joy! Let's have another group tape their balloons above**

### POWER POINTERS

Locate a recording of "Peace Like a River" to sing with kids during the next several weeks. What a timeless song of serenity!

the center line to remind us of the purpose of Jesus' sacrifice on the cross and how it gives us hope and peace. Help kids add their balloons, forming the top part of a cross shape.

Say: **Wow! Just think of God's plan and purpose in bringing us peace. He went to a lot of trouble, heartache, and sacrifice for us, didn't he? But the Lord didn't stop there! Jesus brings us special presents or gifts too. Let's read and see what those special gifts are.** Invite two volunteers to read aloud John 14:27a; Philippians 4:7; and Colossians 3:15. Then ask:

★ **What did Jesus leave us and give to us?**

★ **In what ways is Jesus' peace a gift to us?**

★ **What are we to do with the peace Jesus gave us?**

Say: **Jesus gave us his peace, and he wants that peace to rule in our hearts and guard our minds against sadness, doubt, and troubles. Jesus freely gives us a perfect present of peace when we accept him into our lives and follow him. Now that's what I call a "peace" of heaven! Jesus came to love and forgive us and to give us peace that can never be taken away from the hearts of those who love him. Christ's peace is a gift that lasts forever! Let's add the remaining balloons to the cross to remind us how Jesus' peace is perfect and can never be taken away.**

After the last balloons are added, say: **Jesus had great peace in his life because he obeyed and loved God. Jesus had great peace because he was willing to be used by God and because he used his awesome love to serve us. And Jesus wants us to have his peace as well. Let's make peaceful pictures that will help us focus on the peace that Jesus brings into our lives.**

## THE MESSAGE IN MOTION

Before class, collect magazines with beautiful color pictures of outdoor scenes. *National Geographic* and scenic travel magazines are good choices. Each child will need a picture at least 6-inches square. Photocopy the Peace poem on page 26 for each child.

Let children choose peaceful outdoor scenes from a selection of outdoor and travel magazines. Scenes of mountains, beaches, forests, or meadows make especially pleasing pictures. When a picture is chosen, mount it on heavy cardboard or poster board. (For the best results, glue the picture to a piece of foam board.) Let children use poster board to add shutters. On the

shutters, have kids write John 14:27a: "Peace I leave with you; my peace I give you." As kids work, remind them that we are given Jesus' peace through his forgiveness and love and through our hope of eternal life with him. Ask kids to describe what peace inside their hearts feels like.

When the peaceful scenes are complete, let kids find a place in the room to set their pictures. Distribute the Peace poems and read the poem aloud as kids fill in the blanks to complete the poem. Use the following suggestions as needed to fill in the blanks.

*Line 1: Fill in a type of flower.*

*Line 2: Fill in a noun such as snowflakes or clouds.*

*Line 3: Fill in two adverbs such as mighty, tall, or strong.*

*Line 4: Fill in two adverbs that describe a serence river.*

*Line 5: Fill in a noun that might look like a cloud.*

Then take turns reading the poems aloud as kids view the scenic picture gallery. (If there is time, sing "Peace Like a River.")

Say: **Jesus had peace through God and through God's love. He knew that God's power brings us peace, hope, and joy. Let's review our Mighty Memory Verse, which teaches us even more about peace and where it comes from. Then later, we'll return to our scenic pictures to discover the peace there is in being still before God.**

## SUPER SCRIPTURE

Be sure that you have the newsprint with the Mighty Memory Verse from last week and that the verse is marked with red and yellow markers to indicate the two things we do and the one that God does. Tape the verse to the door or wall for kids to read.

Gather kids by the Mighty Memory Verse and repeat the verse three times aloud. (If you have older kids, introduce the extra-challenge verse now.) Point to the newsprint and ask kids to tell what the red and yellow highlighting stands for, then remind them that this verse teaches two things we're to do (red) and one thing God promises to do for us (yellow).

Say: **Remember last week when we explored how obeying God brings us peace? The word *submit* means nearly the same as the word *obey*. But when we submit to God, we give up our will to him. That means we don't obey stubbornly or grudgingly but cheerfully and willingly. We're to submit to God and to be at peace with him.** Ask:

★ **Why do we want to submit to God?**

★ **What might happen if we don't listen to God or if we choose to disobey him?**

★ **In what ways is being at peace with God the same thing as accepting his will for us without arguing?**

★ Why does God prosper—or bless—us when we submit to him?

Say: **When we submit to God and are at peace with him, God brings prosperity to us. That means God blesses us in many ways, such as through good health, happiness, riches, or having loving families. I'm sure you can think of lots of ways God has already blessed you! And one of those ways is through peace in Jesus. Let's give thanks to God for his blessings of peace through Christ.**

# A **POWERFUL** PROMISE

Have kids sit in a circle. Say: **We've been learning a lot about peace today and how Jesus gave us his peace through the sacrifice of love he made on the cross. We've discovered how Jesus' peace brought us forgiveness and love and the hope of eternal life. We know that Jesus' death and resurrection give us hope in eternal life and great joy because we can be forgiven of our sins. Through this hope and joy, we find peace.**

**Did you know that Jesus had great peace when he went away from his disciples and found quiet places to pray? Jesus knew he could be close to God when he was still and quiet, and in that heavenly stillness, Jesus could peacefully pray to his Father in heaven. We can find peace in the same way. Quietly go and sit in front of your peaceful scene. Then think out a quiet prayer in your heart to thank God for providing us with peace through Jesus.**

Allow several minutes for kids to focus on their peaceful scenes and silently pray to God. Then quietly say "amen." Say: **Take your peaceful scene home and place it in a spot where you can be alone and at peace as you pray and remember that Jesus himself is our peace.**

End with this responsive good-bye:

Leader: **May Jesus' peace be with you forever.**

Children: **And also with you!**

Distribute the Power Page! take-home papers as kids are leaving. Thank kids for coming and encourage them to pray beside their peaceful scenes during the week.

# PEACE POEM

If peace was a flower, it would be a _____, blooming bright and sure.

If peace was a dove, its feathers would be the color of _____, sailing light and pure.

If peace was a mountain, it would be _____ and _____ as could be.

If peace was a river, it would be _____ and _____ flowing out to sea.

If peace was a cloud, it would look like a _____ in the sky above—

But the peace that is ours from Jesus is perfect peace born of his love!

# POWER PAGE!

## Jesus' Perfect Present

Fill in the words to John 3:16 to discover the perfect present Jesus gives us.

For God so _ _ _ _ _ the world
⭐

that he gave his one _ _ _ only Son,
♣

that whoever _ _ _ _ _ _ _ _
✓

in him shall not _ _ _ _ _ _
♥

but have eternal life.

_ _ _ C _
♥ ✓ ♣ ⭐

## PEACE PILLOW

Decorate a small, solid-colored pillow using squirty fabric paints, glow-in-the-dark paints, and bright braid or trim. Create peaceful scenes such as stars, waves, flowers, or praying hands. Set aside time each day to sit or lie down with your Peace Pillow and think about the joyous hope, peace, and love Jesus brings you!

Fill-'em-In

Try This!

**Complete the Mighty Memory Verse, then fit the words into the puzzle.**

_ _ _ _ _ _ _ to _ _ _ and be
_ _ _ _ _ _ _ with him; in
this _ _ _ _ _ _ _ _ _ _ _ _
_ _ _ _ _ _ _ _ to _ _ _.

Job 22:21

S

O

# A SPIRIT OF PEACE

## When we're led by the Holy Spirit, we find peace.

John 14:15-17
Romans 8:6, 9, 14
Galatians 5:22, 23
Ephesians 4:3

### SESSION SUPPLIES

★ Bibles
★ white tissue paper
★ clear sandwich bags
★ construction paper
★ tape & scissors
★ markers
★ white twist-tie wires
★ olive branches (Russian olive)
★ photocopies of the Whiz Quiz (page 36) and the Power Page! (page 35)

## MIGHTY MEMORY VERSE

Submit to God and be at peace with him; in this way prosperity will come to you. Job 22:21

*(For older kids who need an extra challenge, add in Isaiah 48:22: "'There is no peace,' says the LORD, 'for the wicked.'")*

## SESSION OBJECTIVES

During this session, children will
★ understand that Jesus sent us the Holy Spirit
★ realize that the Holy Spirit helps us
★ explore what being led by God's Spirit means
★ learn that trusting the Holy Spirit brings us peace

## BIBLE BACKGROUND

Ask people if they'd rather be viewed by others as a leader or a follower and most would probably choose "leader." But just as Ecclesiastes 3 teaches, there's a time for everything. Being a strong leader for God is wonderful. Yet the Bible teaches us that it's just as important to be led as it is to lead—especially when that leader is the Holy Spirit.

When we're led by the Spirit of God, things just seem to fall into place as they should and, just as the Bible tells us, peace reigns in our hearts and lives. No wonder Romans 8:14 tells us that when we're led by the Spirit, we become children of God! Use this lesson to help kids realize that being a follower can be every bit as important as being a leader—especially when they're following the leading of the Holy Spirit!

# POWER focus

Place clear sandwich bags, twist-tie wires, and white tissue paper in three different parts of the room. Invite kids to find partners or helpers for this activity and explain that today they'll be making something special with the aid of their helpers. Say: **When I say, "go," you must work with your helper to stuff two clear sandwich bags with white tissue paper so the bags are plump. Then close the bags using twist-tie wires. Sound easy? Well, there is a catch! You may each use only one of your hands as you prepare your sandwich bags! When you and your helper have stuffed and sealed two bags, find a place to sit.**

When all the bags have been stuffed, ask:

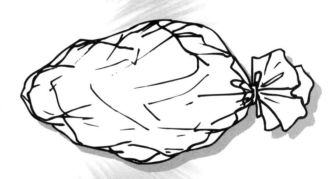

★ **In what ways did it help to have a helper helping you?**

★ **Would it have been easy to stuff the bags alone? Explain.**

★ **When are times you might need help to accomplish something?**

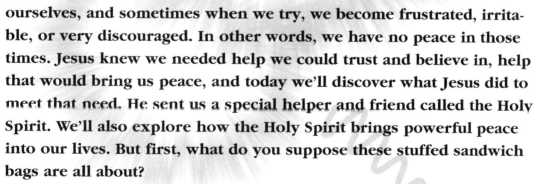

Say: **We can't do everything by ourselves, and sometimes when we try, we become frustrated, irritable, or very discouraged. In other words, we have no peace in those times. Jesus knew we needed help we could trust and believe in, help that would bring us peace, and today we'll discover what Jesus did to meet that need. He sent us a special helper and friend called the Holy Spirit. We'll also explore how the Holy Spirit brings powerful peace into our lives. But first, what do you suppose these stuffed sandwich bags are all about?**

Allow time for kids to tell their ideas, then say: **People didn't understand what the Holy Spirit was all about either—that is, until they saw what the Spirit does and felt the Holy Spirit's peace. Then they knew that when we're led by the Holy Spirit, there is great help and peace! You'll discover what your stuffed bags are as we go through our lesson and as they turn into reminders that the Holy Spirit brings us perfect** peace. Now let's learn a bit more about the Holy Spirit and how the Spirit leads us.

## THE **MIGHTY** MESSAGE

Before class, cut five white construction-paper feather shapes for each child. (See margin illustration.) Layer paper to cut multiple feathers simultaneously. Be sure you have a marker for each child.

Place the white feathers in a pile in the center of the floor, but don't tell kids what the shapes represent. Have kids sit in a circle around the paper feathers. Distribute the markers and have kids hold their stuffed bags. Say: **Let's begin by learning who the Holy Spirit is. I'll read a few verses and then ask some questions. When you think you know an answer, hold your stuffed bag in the air.** Read aloud John 14:15-17 and 16:13. Then ask:

★ **Who sent us the Holy Spirit?**

★ **Why did Jesus send the Holy Spirit to be with us?**

★ **In what ways does the Holy Spirit guide our lives? teach us? draw us closer to God?**

Say: **Jesus sent us the Holy Spirit to be our Counselor, helper, and friend. And Jesus sent the Holy Spirit to be our peace too. When we are led by the Spirit, we find peace. I'll read several verses— when you know what it means to be led by the Holy Spirit, hold your stuffed bag over your heart.**

Read aloud Romans 8:6, 9, 14; Galatians 5:22, 23; and Ephesians 4:3. Then ask:

★ **How does the Holy Spirit lead us?**

★ **How do we act when we're led by the Spirit?**

★ **What good fruit do we have in our lives through the Holy Spirit?**

### POWER POINTERS

Help kids discover more about the Holy Spirit by looking up his other names: Counselor (John 14:16); Spirit of truth (John 14:17); Spirit of God (Matthew 3:16); Spirit of holiness (Romans 1:4).

★ **How do these good things bring us peace?**

Say: **When we're led by the Holy Spirit and follow him, he fills our lives with good things such as joy, love, gentleness, kindness, and self-control. That means we don't live for sinful things; instead, we find peace. Isaiah 48:22 says that "there is no peace for the wicked," but when we're led by the Holy Spirit, we have perfect, powerful peace in our hearts and lives!**

Have each child pick up five white shapes, then say: **Let's list the good components of peace that the Holy Spirit helps us have from Galatians 5:22, 23.** Have kids write two of the fruits of the Spirit on each paper shape. On the last shape, also write the reference (love/joy, peace/patience, kindness/goodness, faith-fulness/gentleness, self-control/Galatians 5:22, 23).

When the "feathers" are fin-ished, say: **Wow! Just look at how the Spirit leads us! When we have love, kind-ness, faithfulness, self-control, patience, joy, goodness, and gentle-ness in our lives, of course we will find heavenly peace. And just think! When we're led by the Holy Spirit, we're called children of God. Matthew 5:9 says, "Blessed are the peace-makers, for they will be called sons of God." That's an awesome thing to be, isn't it? Let's play a quick game to remind us of the good things we find when we're led by the Holy Spirit.**

## THE MESSAGE IN MOTION

Have kids get back with the helpers they had in the Power Focus activity and place their paper feathers and stuffed bags on the floor in front of them. Set several rolls of clear tape in the center of the room. Explain that in this helping relay, you'll call out two fruits of the Spirit. Kids must locate those particular shapes and rush to get two pieces of tape. Then you'll tell kids where to tape the shapes on their stuffed bags. Remind kids that since they have special helpers, they can only use one hand in the relay!

Call out the following directions:

★ "Love and joy" (*tape a feather to one side of the bag*)

★ "peace and patience" *(tape a feather to the other side of the bag)*

★ "kindness and goodness" *(tape a feather to the twist-tie end of the bag)*

★ "faithfulness and gentleness" *(tape a feather to the twist-tie end of the bag)*

★ "self-control" *(tape a feather to the twist-tie end of the bag)*

When the feathers are attached, say: **Your shapes are beginning to come together! Remember, people didn't understand who the Holy Spirit was until they saw what he could do and experienced the peace he brings. As you watch your projects change, you'll soon understand what they are, too, and how they remind us of the special friend Jesus sent to bring us peace! Let's set aside our projects for a moment as we review our Mighty Memory Verse about heavenly peace.**

## SUPER SCRIPTURE

Before this activity, tape the newsprint with Job 22:21 on it to the door or wall. You'll also need a small section of olive branch for each child. Use Russian olive trees and pinch off 2-inch portions of the branches with leaves attached.

Have kids repeat Job 22:21 two times as they look at the newsprint and then one time without looking. Then cover up sections of the verse and challenge volunteers to repeat the entire verse. (If you have older kids, review the extra-challenge verse at this time.) When everyone who wants a turn has had one, say: **This Scripture verse teaches us that through obeying God we find peace and prosperity. In other words, when we obey God and are at peace with him, God blesses us greatly.** Ask:

★ **In what ways is the Holy Spirit a blessing in our lives?**

★ **How does God work through the Holy Spirit to bring us peace? help us serve God?**

★ **How does being led by the Holy Spirit help us obey God?**

Say: **When we're led by the Holy Spirit, we obey God. And what happens when we obey? We find peace!** Distribute the small olive branches, then say. **These are olive branches, and they're a symbol of peace. Let's add these olive branches to our projects. But first, we need to make beaks and eyes. Now do you know what we're making?** Let kids tell their ideas, then say: **We're making doves! Doves are another symbol of peace—and they also symbolize the Holy Spirit in the Bible.**

Help kids cut out construction-paper beaks and tape them in place on their stuffed bags. Tape the olive branches next to the beaks. Use markers to add eyes (or make eyes from construction paper). Say: **We need to add one more part to our doves. Let's form a circle and discover what that part is.**

# A **POWERFUL** PROMISE

Before class, cut out a small, red paper heart for each child. Be sure to have tape ready.

Gather kids in a circle and say: **We've learned today that the Holy Spirit was sent by Jesus to help us and to bring us peace. We've discovered that when we're led by the Spirit, we're children of God and have his perfect peace. And we've worked on our Mighty Memory Verse, which teaches us to submit to God and that he will prosper us. Job 22:21 says** (pause and encourage kids to repeat the verse with you), **"Submit to God and be at peace with him; in this way prosperity will come to you."**

Hand each child a paper heart. Say: **These hearts remind us that when we know, love, and follow the Holy Spirit, he will make our hearts full of peace. Let's tell the Holy Spirit we want to be led by him. As you tape the heart to your dove, say, "Please lead me with your peace and power, Holy Spirit."**

When all the construction-paper hearts are in place on the doves, say: **During the past few weeks we have learned that peace comes from God, from Jesus, and from the Holy Spirit. In the weeks that follow, we will discover how we can be God's peacemakers and help bring peace all around the world.**

Before kids leave, allow five or ten minutes to complete the Whiz Quiz from page 36. If you run out of time, be sure to complete this page first thing next week. The Whiz Quiz is an invaluable tool that allows kids, teachers, and parents see what kids have learned in the previous three weeks.

End with this responsive good-bye:

Leader: **May God fill you with all joy and peace as you trust in him through the Holy Spirit** (adapted from Romans 15:33).

Children: **And also you!**

Distribute the Power Page! take-home papers as kids are leaving. Thank children for coming and encourage them to trust the Holy Spirit to lead them in the coming week.

# POWER PAGE!

## SPIRIT LEADER!

We develop these good things in our lives when we're *led* by the Holy Spirit!

___ ___ ___   ___ ___ ___ ___   ___ ___ ___ ___ ___
✧ ● ➳   ❑ ● ✸ ✓   ✯ ✓ ✡ ✤ ✓

___ ___ ___ ___ - ___ ___ ___ ___ ___ ___ ___
✞ ✓ ❑ ✱   ✤ ● ◆ ♥ ■ ● ❑

___ ___ ___ ___ ___ ___ ___ ___
✪ ✖ ◆ ➌ ◆ ✓ ✞ ✞

___ ___ ___ ___ ___ ___ ___ ___
✯ ✡ ♥ ✖ ✓ ◆ ✤ ✓

| A | C | D | E | F | I | J | K | L |
|---|---|---|---|---|---|---|---|---|
| ✡ | ✤ | ➌ | ✓ | ✱ | ✖ | ✧ | ✪ | ❑ |

| N | O | P | R | S | T | V | Y |
|---|---|---|---|---|---|---|---|
| ◆ | ● | ✯ | ■ | ✞ | ♥ | ✸ | ➳ |

## Dove Salad

***Try this delicious salad for dinner!***

**You'll need:**

- ★ drained pear halves
- ★ shredded coconut
- ★ lettuce leaves
- ★ raisins
- ★ a carrot
- ★ bananas

**For each salad:**

1. Place a lettuce-leaf nest on a plate and lay a pear "dove" in the nest.
2. Peel and slice a banana lengthwise. Cut the halves into six sections and place them beside the dove as wings.
3. Add raisin eyes and a tiny carrot beak.

## SCRAMBLER

**Unscramble the words to Job 22:21 and write them in the correct spaces.**

| | |
|---|---|
| Smbiuvt | nda |
| ta | acpee |
| htis | yaw |
| mih | potrsspreyi |
| uoy | meco |

______ to God ___ be __ _____ with ___; in ____ way __________ will ____ to ___.   Job 22:11

# WHIZ QUIZ

**Match up the correct ending to each statement to make it true.**

✴ There is no peace                                    he will give us peace.

✴ If we obey God,                                       through Jesus' sacrifice of love.

✴ We have peace and hope                               we're led by the Spirit.

✴ Jesus gave us                                        for the wicked.

✴ We find peace when                                   his peace.

## AIM THE ARROWS

**Draw arrows to place the words in their correct positions to complete the Mighty Memory Verse. The first word has been done for you.**

Submit        with        to        at        be

God

Submit _____ _____ and __ __

with

_____ _____ _____ him; __ _____ __ __

_____ will _____ __ __ _____,

prosperity

_____ 22:___

this

way

in

to

peace        come        21        Job        you

# AT PEACE WITH OUR FAMILIES AND FRIENDS

Let the peace of Christ rule
in your hearts, since as
members of one body
you were called to peace.
And be thankful.
Colossians 3:15

# FAMILY FORGIVENESS

**True peace includes a spirit of forgiveness.**

Genesis 50:17-21
Ephesians 4:32
Colossians 3:13, 14
James 3:17, 18

## SESSION SUPPLIES

★ Bibles
★ construction paper
★ markers, scissors, & glue
★ small boxes (one per child)
★ small rolls of tape (one per child)
★ a white crayon
★ aluminum foil
★ newsprint & masking tape
★ photocopies of Colossians 3:15 (page 127)
★ photocopies of the Tools of Peace patterns (page 123)
★ photocopies of the Power Page! (page 45)

## MIGHTY MEMORY VERSE

Let the peace of Christ rule in your hearts, since as members of one body you were called to peace. And be thankful. Colossians 3:15

## SESSION OBJECTIVES

During this session, children will
★ discover that peace comes from forgiveness
★ learn that Jesus wants us to forgive others just as he forgave us
★ explore ways to handle family disagreements
★ understand that they can be peacemakers in their families

## BIBLE BACKGROUND

You've probably heard that charity begins at home. But if we think of charity as a function of the heart and not just the hands or pocketbook, we realize that forgiveness begins at home too. Being charitable, merciful, considerate, non-judgmental, loving, and forgiving can be the toughest when we're dealing with the people who share our homes and lives. It's often easier to forgive a stranger than a sibling or a spouse for even the most trivial of disagreements. But God wants us to live "in peaceful dwelling places, in secure homes, in undisturbed places of rest" (Isaiah 32:18). Isn't it wonderful that God directs us to have charitable hearts and forgiving spirits so *peace* can begin at home too?

Kids are often the most deeply affected family members when disagreements, disputes, and contentions arise, especially among their siblings. Use this lesson to help kids realize that disagreements will happen but that God provides healthy ways of making and regaining peace through forgiveness and love.

## POWER FOCUS

Before class, write the words to the song below on newsprint (or copy the words to make an overhead transparency). Tape the words to a wall or door for kids to read as they sing and become familiar with the song.

Welcome kids and gather them by the words to the song. Lead kids in singing the song to the tune of B-I-N-G-O. As you sing, repeat the song several times, clapping in place of the letters in the word *peace*. Save the song words to use during the upcoming weeks.

*P-E-A-C-E*
(Sing to the tune of B-I-N-G-O)
*I have peace down in my soul*
*That gives me hope and makes me whole!*
*P-E-A-C-E!*
*P-E-A-C-E!*
*P-E-A-C-E!*
*A peacemaker's my goal!*

After singing the song, say: **Wow! That song gives me energy to be a real peacemaker! Just like the song says, being peacemakers is our goal. Give high fives to the other peacemakers around you, then we'll have a quick review of what we've been busy learning.** Allow a few moments as kids greet each other with high fives. Then say: **Now let's see who remembers what we've been learning the past few weeks.** Ask:

★ **Who brings us peace?** (God, Jesus, the Holy Spirit)

★ **How does obeying God bring us peace?**

★ **How does accepting Jesus into our lives bring us hope and peace?**

★ **In what ways does being led by the Spirit bring us peace?**

Then say: **We've learned that obedience to God brings peace, that through Jesus' death and resurrection we have peace and hope, and that by being led by God's Spirit we find peace. Now we'll spend a few** weeks discovering the "tools of peace" and how we can put them to work with our families and friends. Today we'll be discovering that peace in our families begins with forgiveness. We'll learn that we can forgive our family members just as Jesus forgave us. And we'll begin learning a great new Mighty Memory Verse that tells us what needs to be in our hearts as peacemakers.

Right now, we're going to follow in some very important footsteps as we discover the footsteps of forgiveness.

## THE **MIGHTY** MESSAGE

Before class, cut out six black construction-paper footprints by enlarging and using the pattern in the margin. Use a white crayon to write one each of the following on the footprints: peace-loving, considerate, merciful, sincere, impartial or fair, and loving. Tape the footsteps in the above order across the wall going from left to right. You'll also need to cut out a large construction-paper cross, but set it aside until later in the activity.

Gather kids and ask them to tell about times they may have had disagreements with their family members and how they solved the problems. Then say: **The Bible tells us a powerful story about Joseph, whose brothers were very mean and tried to hurt him. But God had chosen Joseph to fulfill a great plan for God's people, so he protected Joseph. However, later in life things still weren't quite right between Joseph and his brothers. Listen**

## POWER POINTERS

Begin a special class and let kids be Mentors of Peace (MPs). When disagreements arise in class, let kids use their Tools of Peace to find peaceful solutions.

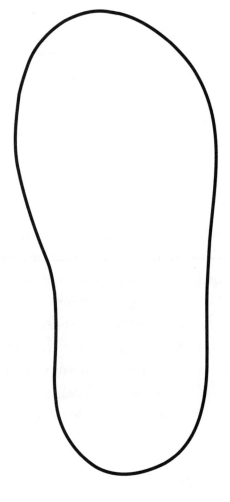

**to how the family problems were solved.** Read aloud Genesis 50:17-21, then ask:

★ **What did Joseph's brothers do to solve the problem?** (They asked for forgiveness.)

★ **How did Joseph react when his brothers requested his forgiveness?** (He accepted and was kind to them.)

★ **What might have happened if Joseph had held a grudge or didn't want to forgive his family?**

Say: **We can learn a very important lesson from Joseph and his brothers. When we have family troubles, it's important to ask for forgiveness. And it's just as important to accept forgiveness. When things aren't right in our families and there are disagreements and misunderstandings, forgiveness really counts! Let's take some big steps in discovering the footsteps to forgiveness and peace.**

Have kids line up at the end of the room opposite the wall with the footsteps or about eight giant steps away from the wall. Then say: **I'll read a few Scripture verses while you listen for words that can help us be forgiving peacemakers.** Read aloud James 3:17, 18 and Colossians 3:13, 14. Then ask:

★ **Why does it take great wisdom to be a peacemaker?**

★ **How do values like sincerity, love, being considerate, and showing mercy help us make peace?**

★ **Why do you think love is the most powerful tool of peace we have?**

Say: **These verses teach us about the importance of forgiveness and what steps we go through in offering and accepting forgiveness to make peace. Let's read the steps aloud as you take a giant step with each word.** Read the first word on the paper footstep aloud and wait for kids to take their giant steps before reading the next word.

When all the steps have been taken, say: **You took many steps. Can you tell me where they led?** Pause for a moment, then tape the paper cross to the wall beside the last footstep. Say: **Yes, the steps lead to forgiveness, but they also lead to the cross of Jesus. You see, Jesus walked these same footsteps for us when he walked with the cross to die for the forgiveness of our sins. These steps in forgiveness lead to Jesus and remind us that we can forgive others just as Jesus forgave us.** Read aloud Ephesians 4:32, then say: **Our families need our forgiveness as much as we need theirs. In this way, we can find peace with those whom we love and live alongside. Forgiveness is one tool of peace. Let's see what some of the other tools are.**

## THE MESSAGE IN **MOTION**

Before class, photocopy the Tools of Peace pattern page on stiff paper for each child. Cut out the Tools of Peace labels and measuring tapes. Kids will be using these patterns for the next several weeks, so keep them in a folder to use as you go. Be sure you have small, inexpensive tape dispensers for each child. (If you prefer, purchase small rolls of colorful electrical tape instead. They come five or six rolls to a package.) If your markers won't write on the tape dispensers, use masking tape so kids can label their tools (or use permanent markers instead).

Hand each child a small box and a Tools of Peace label. (Cover the boxes with construction paper if they have printing on them.) Have kids work in pairs to color the labels, then glue them to the fronts of their tool-kit boxes. If there's time, decorate the edges of the labels and the tool-kits. As kids work, visit about times they might have been a peacemaker in their families and what they did to make or keep peace. Remind kids that we find peace through God, Jesus, and the Holy Spirit and that they provide us the tools to use in making peace.

When the tool-kits are complete, say: **You'll be keeping and using your Tools of Peace kits for the next several weeks, but first you need some tools to go inside! We'll start with the "Tool of Forgiveness."** Hand each child the measuring-tape pattern. Have kids cut out the picture, cover the tape case with aluminum foil, and color the tape portion yellow or gray.

As kids work, say: **This special measuring ruler reminds us of two things. First, we want Jesus to be the ruler of our hearts. And second, we can go the "extra measure" to offer and accept forgiveness in our families. That means that we don't hold grudges or keep score when someone does something wrong. We forgive and forget without measure or limit. The Tool of Forgiveness is the first tool of peace in your kit.** Direct kids to label the measuring tapes with the word "forgiveness" along the tape portion.

Then say: **The next tool is the "Tool of Love."** Hand kids the small tape dispensers to add to their kits. **The tape reminds us of the way love helps us stick together and how love can mend broken hearts. When we love**

Jesus and others, we find peace. That's why the Tool of Love is the second tool of peace in our tool-kits. Label the tape dispensers with the word "love." Then ask:

★ How can the Tool of Forgiveness help when a family member calls you a mean name or says something unkind to you?

★ How can the Tool of Love help when a family member feels hurt?

Say: Next week we'll add more important Tools of Peace to our kits and learn more ways to use them with our families and friends. Right now, let's see how learning God's Word can be another tool of peace! Set the tool-kits aside until next week. Be sure kids' names are on the boxes.

## SUPER SCRIPTURE

Before class, copy the Scripture strip for Colossians 3:15 from page 127 (one for each child) and cut out the verses. Enlarge and copy the rebus verse in the margin on news-print. This week younger kids will work on the first half of the verse ("Let the peace of Christ rule in your hearts…"), while older kids will learn the entire verse. Tape the

newsprint verse to the wall or door for kids to see. Keep the verse to use for the next few weeks.

Gather kids by the verse and repeat the verse three times as you point to the pictures. Then invite volunteers to come forward to repeat the verse as they point to the pictures in the rebus. Say: What a beautiful Scripture verse this is! It tells us exactly who needs to rule our hearts if we're to be peacemakers! Ask:

★ Who must rule our hearts? Why?

★ How does Jesus' peace help us find peace in our own lives?

Say: Jesus' peace is perfect and pure, and he wants to give us that peace. Remember when we learned that Jesus said, "Peace I leave with you; my peace I give you" (John 14:27)? **Jesus can give us his peace when we let him rule our hearts! That's pretty awesome, isn't it? And just think of how peaceful and wonderful it is when we let Jesus' peace rule our families!**

Repeat the verse two more times, then distribute the Scripture strips for kids to take home to learn during the week. Say: **Let's offer Jesus a prayer of thanks for giving us his peace to help in our families and to rule our own hearts.**

# A **POWERFUL** PROMISE

Have kids sit in a circle and ask for a moment of silence, then say: We've learned today that peace in our families begins with the willingness to forgive and to be forgiving. **We've discovered that God gives us tools we can use to make peace in our families and with others. And we began learning a Mighty Memory Verse that says** (pause and encourage kids to repeat the verse with you), **"Let the peace of Christ rule in your hearts," Colossians 3:15.**

Hold up the Bible and say: **Because we know that peace begins with being forgiving, we want to have an attitude of forgiveness with our families. In this way, we become the kind of peacemakers God desires us to be. Let's pass the Bible around the circle and, when it reaches you, say, "Lord, help me be a forgiving peacemaker in my family and with others."** Pass the Bible until everyone has had a chance to hold it. Then close with a prayer thanking Jesus for ruling our hearts with love and forgiveness.

End by reading Isaiah 32:18 and by repeating this responsive good-bye:
Leader: **May you always be forgiving peacemakers.**
Children: **And also you!**
Distribute the Power Page! take-home papers as kids are leaving. Thank children for coming and encourage them to look for ways to be forgiving in their families this week.

# POWER PAGE!

## WISE FOOTSTEPS

**Draw matching lines from the footsteps to the correct lines to complete James 3:17.**

Wisdom that comes from

heaven is first of all

_____; then _____,

_____, _____, full of

_____ and _____,

_____ and _____.

pure

mercy

sincere

impartial

considerate

submissive

peace-loving

good fruit

---

 **Bound-in-Love Bread**

Make this simple loaf of bread lovingly to share with your family. Invite a grown-up family member to help with the fun!

**Whatcha Need:**
★ a tube of refrigerator biscuits
★ a nonstick cookie sheet
★ melted butter    ★ cinnamon sugar

**Whatcha Do:**
**(1)** Preheat the oven to 375 degrees. **(2)** Divide biscuits into 3 groups of 3 biscuits + 1 extra. **(3)** Knead 3 biscuits together, then roll the dough into a "rope." Repeat with other groups. **(4)** Braid the 3 ropes on the cookie sheet. **(5)** Form a heart shape with the extra and place it on the braid. **(6)** Brush loaf with melted butter and cinnamon sugar. **(7)** Bake 20 minutes or until golden brown. Mmm good!

---

*Use the word bank to supply the words to Colossians 3:15, then fill in the letters below to see what Jesus brings us.*

## Word Bank Wonder

_ _ _ the _ _ _ _ _ _ of _ _ _ _ _ _
                              3

_ _ _ in _ _ _ _ _ _ _ _ _ _ _,
2        5

since as _ _ _ _ _ _ _ _ _ _ one body
              7    4  6

you were _ _ _ _ _ _ _ to _ _ _ _ _.
                            1

J_ _ _ _ _ _ _ _ng _ f_ _g_v_n_ _ _.
 1 4 5 4  7 2 3  4  6 2 3 1 1 4 4

| | |
|---|---|
| rule | your |
| members | of |
| peace | peace |
| Let | Christ |
| hearts | called |

# FRIENDLY SERENITY

How we treat our friends has a lot to do with making peace!

Proverbs 14:30; 16:7, 28;
17:9, 17; 26:20
Matthew 22:37-39
1 John 4:7

## SESSION SUPPLIES

★ Bibles
★ kitchen matches
★ metal baking pan
★ white copy paper
★ markers & scissors
★ a cup of water
★ sandpaper
★ aluminum foil
★ glue
★ photocopies of the Paper Pal Proverbs (page 124)
★ photocopies of the Power Page! (page 53)

## MIGHTY MEMORY VERSE

Let the peace of Christ rule in your hearts, since as members of one body you were called to peace. And be thankful. Colossians 3:15

*(For older kids who need an extra challenge, add in James 3:18: "Peacemakers who sow in peace raise a harvest of righteousness.")*

## SESSION OBJECTIVES

During this session, children will
★ learn that friends are gifts from God
★ discover how Jesus wants us to treat our friends
★ realize how envy and gossip bring discord
★ explore ways to keep peace with friends

## BIBLE BACKGROUND

*Make new friends, but keep the old—one is silver and the other's gold!* It's wonderful to make new friends and to reminisce with the old. And it's equally wonderful that God provides us with pointers throughout the Bible about how to keep peace with our friends and acquaintances. Even the best of friendships become strained at times and need peacemaking skills to keep them going and growing.

Kids' number one classroom complaint is often the exaggerated wail of, "I have no friends!" What they're trying to say is, "I know people who I'd like to be friends with, but I don't know how," or "My friend and I are having a fight." Friendship is most certainly a learned skill and must be generously peppered with peacemaking tools to keep friends close. Use this lesson to help kids understand that friendship takes a bit of work and that God will guide their friendships as he shows them ways to keep the peace and love flowing!

# POWER FOCUS

Before class, write the letters P, E, A, C, and E on five sheets of paper. Set the metal baking pan, matches (long, kitchen type), a cup of water, and a 4-inch square of paper on a table.

Welcome kids and hand five kids each a page with a letter on it. Invite the kids to stand in front of the class so they spell out the word *peace*. Then have kids hide the letters. Explain that you'll sing the P-E-A-C-E song from last week (page 39) and, as you sing or clap the letters in the word *peace,* the kids holding the letters will hold them up quickly, then hide them again.

After singing, gather everyone around the table and say: **I'd like to show you something interesting. I have a match and a piece of paper here. What do you think will happen if I light the match, then hold the paper to it?** Allow kids to tell the paper will catch fire and burn. Then say: **Let's see if you're right.** Light the match and let it burn for a five to ten seconds before touching the paper to the fire. When the paper catches fire, drop the match and paper in the metal pan and let the fire burn for a few moments before pouring a bit of water on it.

Say: **That fire really started burning when I added fuel to it! It was burning to start with, but the paper added more fuel to the fire and made it burn even hotter.** Ask:

★ **In what ways is this like speaking mean words to a friend?**

★ **How was the water like bringing peace to an argument?**

Say: **The Bible tells us that without wood a fire will go out and that without gossip and mean words a quarrel will die down and peace can return. Today we'll be taking a close look at how to keep peace with our friends. We'll discover that mean words, gossiping, and jealousy start fights that burn like a fire—and how love and acceptance put out the fire and bring peace back to friends. Let's begin by making some paper pals, then we'll read what the Bible says about making peace with friends.**

# THE **MIGHTY** MESSAGE

Before class, practice folding and cutting out paper dolls according to the directions in the margin. Accordion-fold a piece of white copy paper the long way, making five accordion folds. Cut the long strip in half and make paper dolls using both halves. When opened, you should have two sets of three dolls. Tape the arms together to make a row of six dolls. You'll also need to photocopy the Paper Pal Proverbs from page 124, one copy per child.

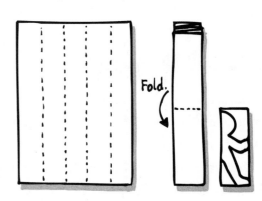

Fold.

Have kids get into small groups of four or five and hand each child a sheet of paper and a pair of scissors. Demonstrate how to make two sets of paper dolls and to tape their arms to make rows of six dolls. Then hand each child a copy of the Paper Pal Proverbs. Have kids cut apart the proverbs, but don't glue them in place yet.

Say: **Now that we have our paper pals, let's see what God says about what we can do or say to our friends as peacemakers. Let's take turns reading these wise proverbs aloud and answering some questions about how they relate to friendships and peace.** Read each proverb aloud, then answer these two questions for each:

★ *What does this proverb teach us about friends?*

★ *How does this proverb help us find peace with our friends?*

When all six proverbs have been read and discussed, say: **Because God is the God of peace, when we obey him we discover peaceful solutions to any problems. God gives us wisdom through his proverbs and teaches us about the value of having good friends as well as how to be peacemakers among our friends. Listen to what Jesus teaches us about loving our friends and being at peace with them.**

Read aloud Matthew 22:37-39, then ask:

## POWER POINTERS

Kids may enjoy bringing in photos of themselves and their friends and making a bulletin-board collage. Title the display: "Good Friends Are Like a 'Peace' of Heaven!"

★ In what ways does keeping peace with our friends express our respect for them? our love for God?

★ In what ways do envy and gossip ruin friendships? How do kind words and help strengthen friendships?

★ How do you want your friends and others to treat you?

★ Do these ways encourage peace? Explain.

Say: **Friends are like wonderful gifts from God! And though we may find ourselves disagreeing with friends and perhaps even arguing with them, we can still respect and love them and can still have peace with them. After all, aren't friends worth it? Glue your proverbs to your paper pals, then write the first name of a friend you have on each paper pal.**

When the proverbs are in place and the friends' names have been added, say: **When you go home, put your paper pals where you'll see them often. Then as you go through the upcoming weeks, read the proverbs and your friends' names and look for ways to encourage peace among yourselves by obeying God's Word.**

**Are you ready to see what Tools of Peace we'll add to our tool-kits today? Then let's get our kits as we discover more about being God's peacemakers!**

## THE MESSAGE IN MOTION

Be sure you have the Tools of Peace patterns from the previous lesson. Today you'll need the magnifying glass. You'll also need to cut a 4-inch square of sandpaper for each child.

When kids have their tool-kits, have them open the kits up and review the two Tools of Peace inside. Ask:

★ **How is the Tool of Love** (tape) **used in making peace?**

★ **Why is it important for a peacemaker to have love?**

★ **How is the Tool of Forgiveness** (measuring tape) **used in making peace?**

★ **Who has forgiven us so that we might forgive others and be peacemakers?**

Say: **Today, we'll add two new Tools of Peace to your kits. The first is the Tool of Mercy.** Hand kids the magnifying-glass pattern and have them cut out the pictures and wrap aluminum foil around the "glass" portion. Write "mercy" on the handles and color them. As kids work, say: **This important tool is used for magnifying things and taking a good, close look at ourselves and being honest if we're treating others as we want to be treated. Are we treating our friends with mercy, compassion, and respect?**

Read Matthew 22:37-39 again, then continue: **Jesus taught us to love God first, then our neighbors and friends as we love ourselves. What an important rule. And the Tool of Mercy is an important tool!**

**The next Tool of Peace is the Tool of Kindness. Just as sandpaper smoothes away rough spots and nicks, our actions and words of kindness smooth away hurt, doubts, and lies and make peace in amazing ways! The Tool of Kindness is one of our most important Tools of Peace.** Have kids write the word "kindness" on the backs of the sandpaper squares.

Then read aloud the following situations kids might find themselves in with their friends. Have kids hold up which Tools of Peace would be helpful and explain why.

★ *You and your friend have been arguing over what game to play.*
★ *Your friend has been gossiping about you, and you're upset.*
★ *Your friend wants you to do something you know is wrong.*
★ *Your best friend broke your favorite toy.*

Say: **You see, these are great tools to use as peacemakers. We know that God, Jesus, and the Holy Spirit are our sources of peace, and now you have tools to use as God's peacemakers. Now let's review God's Word, which is also a powerful tool of peace.** Set aside the tool-kits to use next week.

## SUPER SCRIPTURE

Be sure you have the newsprint with Colossians 3:15 written on it. Repeat the portion of the verse you learned last week three times ("Let the peace of Christ rule in your hearts..."). If you have younger children, let them take turns covering up pictures and words and repeating the verse. If you have older kids, review the entire verse. (If kids are up to the task, introduce the extra-challenge verse at this time.) Repeat the entire verse three times aloud, then ask:

★ **How does having Jesus rule our hearts help calm our hearts and lives?**

★ **Why do you think Jesus gave us his peace?**

★ **Why have we been called to peace? Who has called us?**

Say: **The second portion of this verse reminds us how we are all members of one body—we all belong to Jesus. And it also reminds us that Jesus calls us to peace and to be peacemakers. We're one body of believers, from one family—the family of God. Remember that Matthew 5:9 tells us that we are blessed when we're peacemakers because we are called children of God. And for this, we're truly thankful! Colossians 3:15 reminds us of our heavenly family and of our responsibility as peacemakers. Let's sing the P-E-A-C-E song as we proudly rejoice over being peacemakers in God's family!**

*P-E-A-C-E*

(Sing to the tune of B-I-N-G-O)

*I have peace down in my soul*
*That gives me hope and makes me whole!*
*P-E-A-C-E!*
*P-E-A-C-E!*
*P-E-A-C-E!*
*A peacemaker's my goal!*

After singing the P-E-A-C-E song, say: **I love being part of God's family, and it makes me feel good to know that I have been called to be his peacemaker for my family and friends! Let's end our time together by thanking God for his special gift of friends and by telling God we want to be peacemakers with our friends.** Keep the newsprint verse to use next week.

## A POWERFUL PROMISE

Have kids sit in a circle and ask for a moment of silence, then say: **We've learned today that God gives us good friends and wants us to have** peaceful relationships with them. We've discovered that God gives us words of wisdom in how to treat our friends and that if we obey, we'll find peace with them. We've also learned that gossiping and being jealous of what others have leads to unrest and even fights. And we've worked on the Mighty Memory Verse that tells us to let the peace of Christ rule our hearts. Colossians 3:15 says (pause and encourage kids to repeat the verse with you), **"Let the peace of Christ rule in your hearts, since as members of one body you were called to peace. And be thankful."**

Hold up the Bible and say: **God wants us to honor our friends by treating them with compassion, respect, mercy, and love—values that encourage peace. Let's tell God how much we want to be peacemakers with our friends this week and forever. We'll pass the Bible and take turns holding it. When it's your turn, you can say, "I want to encourage peace among my friends, Lord."** Pass the Bible until everyone has had a chance to hold it.

Close by reading 1 John 4:7, then end with this responsive good-bye:

Leader: **May the Spirit of peace be with you.**

Children: **And also with you!**

Distribute the Power Page! take-home papers as kids are leaving. Thank children for coming and encourage them to read their Paper Pal Proverbs often this week as they seek to be peacemakers among their friends.

# POWER PAGE!

## FRIENDLY Q & A

*Draw lines from the question to the
correct answer. (Use your Bible!)*

Who should we
first love?

loves
(Prov. 17:17)

Who should we
love next?

no gossip
(Prov. 26:20)

What does a friend
do at all times?

your neighbor
(Matt. 22:39)

What makes a
quarrel die down?

God
(Matt. 22:37, 38)

What gives life
to the body?

peaceful hearts
(Prov. 14:30)

## Sweet 'n Sour

Our tongues can tell sweet from sour
with just a taste! Take a taste of the following and tell which is sour or bitter.

♥ unsweetened soft drink mix

♥ vanilla extract    ♥ lemon juice

♥ corn syrup or honey   ♥ cinnamon

♥ brown sugar

How are words to your friends like sweet
and sour tastes? God wants us to speak
sweet words of kindness and love to our
friends. Write an encouraging note to a
friend, then dip a plastic spoon in honey
and dip it in powdered gelatin. Slip the
sweet treat in a sandwich bag and give
the gift and note to a favorite friend!

*Follow the arrows to plug
in the missing letters from
Colossians 3:15.*

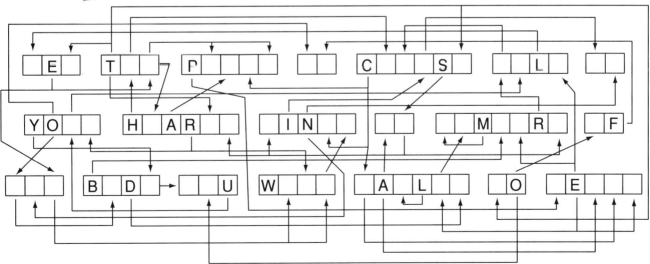

# PEACE OF MIND

We must use God's direction and wisdom when seeking peace.

1 Samuel 25:32-35
Matthew 5:9

## SESSION SUPPLIES

★ Bibles
★ yellow poster board
★ 1-inch-wide rainbow ribbon
★ stapler, scissors, & tape
★ aluminum foil
★ fine-tipped permanent markers
★ self-adhesive gold-foil seals (2-inch diameter)
★ small vanilla wafer-type cookies
★ plastic knives
★ canned icing
★ photocopies of Colossians 3:15 (page 127)
★ photocopies of the Whiz Quiz (page 62) and the Power Page! (page 61)

## MIGHTY MEMORY VERSE

Let the peace of Christ rule in your hearts, since as members of one body you were called to peace. And be thankful. Colossians 3:15

*(For older kids who need an extra challenge, add in James 3:18: "Peacemakers who sow in peace raise a harvest of righteousness.")*

## SESSION OBJECTIVES

During this session, children will
★ learn that all wisdom comes from God
★ realize that wisdom is a powerful peacemaking tool
★ discover how communication helps make peace
★ thank God for giving us his perfect wisdom

## BIBLE BACKGROUND

When was the last time you had a disagreement or an argument with someone? You probably had little trouble communicating your displeasure or irritation during the dispute, but was there good communication *before* the problem arose? Wise communication can stop problems before they get out of hand and is not only helpful but necessary when trying to make peace after the fact. As the Bible both shows and tells us, wisdom and communication, when combined, are powerful peacemaking tools that God directs and supplies when we're open and obedient to him.

Kids are often spontaneous, quick on the draw, and impulsive. As a result, they tend to act and speak without thinking first—and thus are born arguments and irritations that need patient peacemaking skills! Kids need to understand that God gives us wisdom in what to say and that if we're communicating early and effectively, we can avoid many problems and keep peace. Use this lesson to help kids realize that peacemakers seek God's wisdom and rely on him to help them communicate peacefully with others.

# POWER focus

Before class, cut an 18-inch length of rainbow-colored ribbon for each child. Use at least 1-inch-wide ribbon. If you can't find rainbow ribbon, any color will do. (You'll be making cookie medals to share with another class later in the lesson. You may want to cut two more ribbon sections for each child at the same time as you cut ribbon for this activity.)

Gather kids and distribute the ribbons. Explain that these ribbons will be used throughout the lesson but that you'll begin by waving them in time to the P-E-A-C-E song. Encourage kids to hop in place instead of clapping for the letters in the word *peace*.

*P-E-A-C-E*
(Sing to the tune of B-I-N-G-O)
*I have peace down in my soul*
*That gives me hope and makes me whole!*
*P-E-A-C-E!*
*P-E-A-C-E!*
*P-E-A-C-E!*
*A peacemaker's my goal!*

When you're finished singing, have kids hold the ends of each other's ribbons to make a large circle. Say: **Let's open with a quick prayer asking God to give us wisdom as we explore more about being peacemakers.** Pray: **Dear God, we know all wisdom comes from you, and we know there is no peace without obeying your wisdom. Please give us wisdom and understanding as we learn today that wisdom is an important tool in making and keeping peace. Amen.** Have kids drape their ribbons over their shoulders for the time being.

Say: **Today we'll hear an exciting story of how one woman in the Bible made peace and averted an awful war! We'll discover the importance of wisdom and discernment in keeping peace. And we'll see how well you remember the Mighty Memory Verse. Right now, let's learn about this brave and wise woman who stopped a war from happening. You can use your ribbons and Tools of Peace tool-kits to help.**

## THE **MIGHTY** MESSAGE

Before class, tape a 3-foot length of ribbon to the wall. Cut five 4-inch poster-board circles and label them as follows: Nabal, David, Abigail, fighting, and peace. Tape the circle labeled "fighting" to the left end of the ribbon and the "peace" circle on the other end. Set the tape beside the wall.

Have kids gather by the ribbon on the wall and hold their own ribbons. Point to the ribbon on the wall and say: **This ribbon is called the "spectrum of peace." At one end is fighting** (have kids shake their ribbons on the floor to the left), **and at the other is peace** (shake ribbons high and to the right). **We all move along this spectrum every day. Sometimes we feel a bit cranky and might snap at friends or family members. Some days we may be cranky enough to be looking for a fight. But we want to be at the peaceful end where peacemakers should be! We'll use the spectrum of peace to help tell our Bible story, which is found in 1 Samuel and tells about three people: David before he was king, a wealthy shepherd named Nabal, and Nabal's wife Abigail. As I tell the story, you can help by deciding which Tools of Peace Abigail is using and where everyone is along the spectrum of peace.** (Tape the three circles with the names below the center of the ribbon on the wall. You'll be moving the characters as you tell the story.)

**The Bible tells us that Abigail was a beautiful woman and very wise. It also says that Nabal was a surly, cranky man who wasn't very nice in his dealings with friends. Where would Nabal and Abigail be on the**

### POWER POINTERS

Make edible Peace Medallions (from the Message in Motion section) as a service project. Present the medallions to the congregation with cards with Matthew 5:9 on them.

**spectrum of peace?** Invite a child to tape Nabal to the left of center, toward the fighting end, as kids wave their ribbons low and to the left. Tape Abigail off center to the right a bit as kids wave their ribbons high and to the right.

Continue: **David was chosen by God to be the next king of Israel. He and his soldiers had been living out in the wilderness and were tired and hungry and out of food. David kindly asked Nabal for food and supplies. Where would David be on the spectrum of peace for asking nicely for food?** Have a child tape David to the right of center because he asked in a kind way and didn't order Nabal to give him food or go steal it. Wave ribbons to the right.

**But Nabal was angry that someone would dare ask him for help or food! Nabal quickly and rudely said, "No food!" By his answer, would Nabal be closer to peace or fighting?** Have kids explain their answers, then ask kids how Nabal might have responded in a more peacemaking way. Then move Nabal closer to the fighting end of the ribbon and wave the ribbons to the left. **When David heard Nabal's reply, he was very angry! David told his men to draw their swords, for David would battle Nabal. Where would David be on the spectrum of peace now?** Encourage kids to tell that David was close to fighting, then ask how David might have responded differently to keep peace. Move David to the fighting end of the ribbon and wave the ribbons to the left.

**When Abigail heard what had happened and knew that David would make war with Nabal, she jumped into action! First, Abigail took bread, meat, fruit, and grain to David and his hungry men. Which Tool of Peace did she use?** Have kids tell their ideas, then move Abigail a bit closer to the peace end as they wave their ribbons high and to the right. **Next, Abigail asked for David's forgiveness even though she herself had done nothing wrong. Which Tool of Peace did Abigail use?** Again, allow response, then move Abigail beside the peace circle at the end of the ribbon. Wave ribbons to the right.

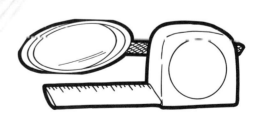

**Although he was angry at Nabal, David listened to Abigail, then he accepted her food and her apologies. David had chosen peace instead of fighting because of wise Abigail! Which Tools of Peace did David use?** Let kids respond, then move David beside the peace circle next to Abigail and wave their ribbons to the right. Ask:

★ **How did wisdom help Abigail make peace between Nabal and David?**

★ **What might have happened if Abigail hadn't made peace?**

★ **What can we learn about peace from Abigail? Nabal? David?**

Say: **Nabal wasn't interested in making peace, and David let his temper run away with him. But Abigail used great wisdom in her peacemaking decisions. She used the Tools of Peace God has given us and prevented an awful war. Abigail was truly a hero—and a great peacemaker! Let's add the last two Tools of Peace that Abigail taught us about to our tool-kits.**

## THE MESSAGE IN MOTION

Make sure you have the last two patterns for the Tools of Peace ready (the hammer and the pliers). Photocopy the Scripture strips for Colossians 3:15 from page 127. You'll need two copies for every child. You'll also need four vanilla wafer-type cookies and two 18-inch lengths of ribbon for each child. (Don't use the ribbons the kids have been waving. You'll use those again later.)

Have kids cut out the hammer and the pliers from their pattern pages. Cover the ends of the hammers and pliers with aluminum foil and color the handles. Label the hammer with the word "wisdom" and the pliers with "communication."

Say: **Abigail used one of the most important Tools of Peace God gives us: wisdom. Abigail thought out the problem and the best way to solve it. Abigail used the wisdom God gave her in deciding how best to make peace between Nabal and David. The Tool of Wisdom helps us nail down the truth and decide the best way to handle a situation peaceably.**

**The other tool Abigail used was the Tool of Communication. Abigail talked to David and communicated with him. This gave David time to think and cool down. Talking things out calmly and peacefully is a powerful tool!** Ask:

★ **How can talking to your friends and families stop problems before they happen?**

Let the peace of Christ rule in your hearts, since as members of one body you were called to peace. And be thankful. Colossians 3:15

★ **In what ways are God's wisdom and our obedience related? How can they work together to bring peace?**

Say: **Abigail took food as an offering of peace to David. Let's make our own fun peace offering for another class to remind them how important it is to seek peace!** Show kids how to ice the flat sides of two wafer cookies, then stick the ends of a length of ribbon in the icing of one cookie. Add the second cookie sandwich-style to make edible, wearable Peace Medallions. Finally, staple or tape a Scripture strip for Colossians 3:15 to each medallion. Have each child make one Peace Medallion to wear and one to share with someone in another class at the end of the lesson. (Make sure you have enough edible medallions for everyone in the other class!)

Say: **Your medallions look good enough to eat! And let's face it—being peacemakers is a sweet thing, isn't it? Learning God's Word is sweet too. Let's see how well you remember the Mighty Memory Verse.**

## SUPER SCRIPTURE

Before class, cut the newsprint containing Colossians 3:15 (from last week) into ten sections. If you have young children, use just the first portion of the verse. If your class is very large, cut the verse into more pieces and form pairs or trios. You'll also need a 2-inch circle of yellow poster board and a gold-foil medallion or starburst for each child.

Repeat Colossians 3:15 aloud three times, then have kids reassemble the verse using the puzzle pieces. Challenge kids to turn their backs to the verse and repeat it without peeking. (If you have older kids, review the extra-challenge verse as well.) Then ask:

★ **Why do we need Jesus ruling our hearts to become good peacemakers?**

★ **How does it help and encourage us to know that all Christians are called to be peacemakers?**

★ **What can you do to let Jesus rule your heart even more?**

Hand each child a yellow poster-board circle. Have kids use fine-tipped permanent markers to write "Let the peace of Christ rule in your hearts" on the backs of the circles. Stick a gold-foil medallion to the front of each circle, then have kids write "Peacemaker" on the gold foil. Staple or tape the ends of the ribbons kids have been waving to the circles to make necklace medallions—but don't wear them yet! Set the medallions aside until the next activity.

Say: **All wisdom comes from God, and he gives us wisdom to use in making peace with our families and friends. Abigail used wisdom in making peace with someone from her family and another person at the same time! It's a good thing God provides direction for us, isn't it? Let's thank God for his wisdom that we can put to work as his peacemakers.**

## A POWERFUL PROMISE

Gather kids in a circle and have them hold their medallions. Say: **We've been learning today that wisdom comes from God and can be used in making peace with our friends and families. We've discovered that wisdom and communication are important tools of peace. Let's bow our heads and thank God for his wisdom.** Pray: **Dear Lord, we know that all wisdom comes from you. Please give us wisdom to know the best ways to bring peace to our families and friends. In Jesus' name, amen.**

Have kids form pairs and hold each other's medallions. Say: **Let's promise to try and bring peace to our families and friends in the coming weeks. Say, "I want to be a peacemaker" as your partner places your medallion around your neck.**

Before kids leave, allow five or ten minutes to complete the Whiz Quiz from page 62. If you run out of time, be sure to do this page first thing next week. The Whiz Quiz is an invaluable tool that allows kids, teachers, and parents see what kids have learned in the previous three weeks.

Close by presenting your edible Peace Medallions to another class. Remind kids that peace comes from the Lord, who calls us to be his peacemakers. Read aloud Matthew 5:9. End with this responsive good-bye:

Leader: **May God's wisdom and peace be with you.**

Children: **And also with you!**

Distribute the Power Page! take-home papers as kids are leaving. Thank children for coming and encourage them to keep their peacekeeping promises to God this week.

# POWER PAGE!

## Peace Makers

Fill in the missing words, then solve the puzzle to show where peace comes from.

Matt. 5:9: Blessed are the peacemakers, for

_ _ _ _ _ will be _ _ _ _ _ _ _ _
    ★           ✓          ◇

_ _ _ _ _ of _ _ _
   ❂        ✖    ❑

James 3:18: Peacemakers who

_ _ _ _ _ _ _ _ _ _ raise a
❸     ✳     ✤        ✝

_ _ _ _ _ _ _ _ of righteousness.
♥    ✺      ➤

*Our peace comes from:*

_ _ _ , J _ _ U _ ,
✖ ❂ ❑    ✝ ❸    ❸

_ _ _ _ _ _ _ _ _ _
♥ ❂ ✓ ★ ❸ ✤ ✳ ✺ ✳ ➤

## High & LOW

Fill in the missing high, low, and in-between letters to complete Colossians 3:15.

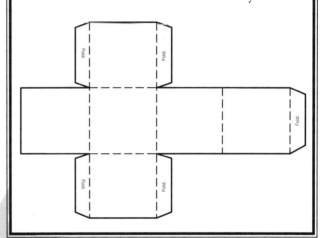

### WISDOM

*Use construction paper to make a six-sided cube. Write one of the words below on each side. Roll the cube each day and look for ways to use this Tool of Peace wisely with your family and friends.*

- ★ forgiveness
- ★ kindness
- ★ communication
- ★ love
- ★ wisdom
- ★ mercy

# WHIZ QUIZ

**Color in T (true) or F (false) to answer the questions.**

➤ Jesus brings us forgiveness of our sins.                     (T)  (F)

➤ All wisdom comes from our teachers.                          (T)  (F)

➤ Friends make peace through gossip and envy.                  (T)  (F)

➤ A friend loves at ALL times.                                 (T)  (F)

➤ We're to love God first, then our neighbors.                 (T)  (F)

➤ It takes wisdom to be a peacemaker.                          (T)  (F)

## Word Bank Wonder

**Use the words from the word banks to complete the MIGHTY MEMORY VERSE.**

**WORD BANK**

peace
members
hearts
body
called
your

**WORD BANK**

Christ
Let
rule
peace
you
since

_____ the _____ of

_____ _____ in _____

_____, _____ as

_____ of one _____

_____ were _____

to _____. Colossians 3:15

# AT PEACE IN THE WORLD

Blessed are the
peacemakers,
for they will be called
sons of God.
Matthew 5:9

# DELIGHTFULLY DIFFERENT

God made a wide variety of people to celebrate.

Isaiah 52:7
Romans 2:10, 11, 10:12, 13
1 Corinthians 12:4-10

## SESSION SUPPLIES

★ Bibles
★ 3-inch-wide yellow satin ribbon & scissors
★ self-adhesive hook-and-loop fastening tape
★ black permanent markers
★ a large manila envelope
★ gold glitter glue
★ postcards (one per child or make your own)
★ colored markers
★ newsprint
★ postage stamps (for postcards)
★ photocopies of Matthew 5:9 (page 127)
★ photocopies of the Power Page! (page 71)

## MIGHTY MEMORY VERSE

Blessed are the peacemakers, for they will be called sons of God. Matthew 5:9

## SESSION OBJECTIVES

During this session, children will
★ understand that God made all people as he chose
★ discover that God doesn't play favorites
★ learn that God honors all people who love him
★ realize that we can live at peace with people different from us

## BIBLE BACKGROUND

Imagine a world in which there was only chocolate to eat. Sound like a delightful dream? Well, maybe for the first few meals. But even the most hard-core chocoholics would probably grow tired of eating the sweet treat within a few days. We celebrate variety in the foods we choose and enjoy. Why, then, is it difficult for many of us to enjoy the wonderful variety of people God has given to share our world? Too often people judge the differences of others as inferior to themselves or view diversity in a divisive way, which leads to intolerance, bigotry, and unrest. God looks beyond the outward differences in people and desires us to do the same. When we respect, accept, and are compassionate to others, we can begin to live in peace.

Kids can be especially cruel when it comes to differences. Taunting remarks, teasing, and bullying are often the result of judging others' differences. Kids need to understand that God wants us to embrace a wide variety of people by carrying his love and peace to them willingly. Use this lesson to help kids recognize that people's differences are part of God's wonderful creation and are to be celebrated.

## POWER FOCUS

Warmly welcome kids and direct them stand at one end of the room. Say: **We know that God made all people, and God made people the way he alone chose! God made us all similar in many ways, but he also made us all special individuals. Let's play a grouping game to see how we're alike and different.**

Give the following directions for grouping kids and have them rush to form the appropriate groups.

★ *Form groups according to your hair color: blonde, brown, black, red, or other.*

★ *Form groups according to eye color: blue, brown, green, hazel, or other.*

★ *Form groups of boys and girls.*

★ *Form groups according to the months that birthdays occur.*

★ *Form groups according to grades in school.*

★ *Form groups according to favorite foods: pizza, hot dogs, spaghetti, or other.*

Say: **That was fun! Now let's form a group of anyone who loves God and wants to be his peacemaker!** Pause as kids all get into one large group, then say: **Now give your group members high fives.**

After the high fives, have kids sit in place. Say: **God made so many different people with so many special traits. Wouldn't it be awful if we all looked and sounded alike? How would we ever tell one another apart? But God in his wisdom made us all similar and yet all different—and God loves each of us just the way we are!**

Today and for the next few weeks, we'll be discovering that we can live in peace with people who are different from us. We'll learn that God doesn't play favorites and loves us all the same. And we'll begin learning a super new Mighty Memory Verse about being peacemakers. But right now, let's make cool peacemaker arm bands as we discover why God wants us to live in peace with all people.

## THE **MIGHTY** MESSAGE

Before class, be sure you have enough 3-inch-wide yellow ribbon for each child to make an arm band. You'll be measuring ribbon loosely around upper arms, then cutting the lengths you need. Kids will then place self-adhesive hook-and-loop fasteners on the ends of the ribbons to secure the bands around their arms.

Help kids measure the yellow ribbon around their arms, add an extra half-inch of length, and cut the ribbon. Then show kids how to stick a 1-inch piece or circle of self-adhesive hook-and-loop fastener at each end of their ribbons. (Hint: stick one piece of fastener at one end of each ribbon, then flip the ribbons over and add the other piece on the opposite end. The ribbons will lie flat against kids' arms this way.)

When everyone has a yellow ribbon, say: **We all know that God is our heavenly Creator and has created all people. When we look around our classroom, around our town, or around the world, we often just look at how people are different from the outside. People notice different sizes and shapes, different hair colors and ways to style hair, different skin and eye colors, and other outside features. But how does God look at us?**

Read aloud 1 Samuel 16:7b, then say: **When God looks at people, he sees their hearts and not their outward differences. And this is how God wants us to see others. Hair, skin, and eye colors don't matter, nor does size or shape or where a person lives. With God, there are no favorites; he loves and blesses those people who love him.** Read aloud Romans 2:11 and 10:12, 13, then ask:

★ **How does it make you feel to know God loves us all?**

### POWER POINTERS

During the next few weeks, kids will be "MPs" (Mentors of Peace). Encourage teachers in other classes to allow MPs to help settle minor disputes or disagreements among kids in their classrooms.

★ **How can looking at people's hearts, not their differences, encourage peace?**

Have kids hold their ribbons, then say: **Look around the room at one another. There's something we all have in common—something other than our love for the Lord!** Guide kids to notice that everyone is holding the same color ribbon, then continue: **We're all holding yellow ribbons. They may be different lengths, but they're the same color. Did you know that the color yellow symbolizes friendship and peace? And the fasteners remind us that when we're connected to Christ, we can live in peace with others just as he desires.**

**God made each of us unique and has given us unique gifts we can use to bring peace to others. Listen to the different gifts God gives us.** Read aloud 1 Corinthians 12:4-10, then say: **During the next few weeks, we'll put our gifts to work to bring peace to others by becoming "MPs" or Mentors of Peace. When there are disagreements or troubles in another class, groups of you will be called to bring peace by helping solve the problems. You have your Tools of Peace tool-kits to use, and now you'll have MP arm bands to wear. Let's write "MP" on the arm bands. Then we'll wear the arm bands and be prepared to bring peace when we're called as peacemakers!**

Have kids write large MPs on their arm bands. Have older kids also write "Mentors of Peace" in small letters below the MP. Use gold glitter glue to draw a heart beside the MP. Encourage other teachers, especially of preschool classes, to call on groups of your kids to help solve problems. Peer mentoring in peaceful solutions is a powerful peacemaking tool, and kids often see solutions that are overlooked by adults.

When the arm bands are done, set them aside to dry. Kids will be able to wear their arm bands next week. Say: **Doesn't it feel great to know you're God's peacemakers? Now let's take the Lord's peace around the world! We can make neat Peacemaker Postcards to send to people who may seem different than we are—but are all loved by God!**

## THE MESSAGE IN MOTION

Before class, purchase inexpensive postcards that show different local scenes. If you have a lot of kids, simply make a 4-by-5-inch pattern and copy your own cards on stiff paper. Add your church's return address to the copied cards or use address labels on the purchased postcards. You'll also need a postage stamp for each child. (Note: You'll be sending out Peacemaker Postcards for the next three weeks. Purchase enough stamps and postcards or make postcards one of the weeks.) Decide where you'll be sending your cards so you can tell kids. (Suggestions are given later in this activity.)

Have kids form small groups and say: **One of the best ways to bring peace around the world is to carry the good news about Jesus! Listen to what the Bible says about bringing good news.**

Read aloud Isaiah 52:7, then ask:

★ **Why is bringing good news a way to encourage peace?**

★ **How can telling others about Jesus encourage them? give them Jesus' peace?**

Say: **Let's carry our own good news about Jesus around the world with Peacemaker Postcards. For the next couple of weeks, we'll be making postcards to send to different countries as ambassadors of peace for God. Today we'll be making and sending Peacemaker Postcards to the people in another area of the world. Remember, the best way to have peace is to offer peace, and that's what our Peacemaker Postcards will do.**

Let children choose scenic cards or use markers to decorate their own. On the note portion of each card, have kids write: "Peace I leave with you; my peace I give you" (John 14:27). Add any other short messages of encouragement or praise for Jesus, then affix a church return-address label and stamp.

Place the cards in a large manila envelope and address it to one of your church missionaries to deliver to the people they're helping or to an affiliated church in your area. If you prefer, send the envelope to:

Youth with a Mission (YWAM)
P.O. Box 3000, Attn: Dept. SF
Lindale, TX 75771

When the cards are complete, say: **We'll make sure these are mailed, and as they're traveling to their destinations, you can have peace in your hearts knowing your words of encouragement will brighten someone's day with Jesus' love! Right now, let's show God how much we love his Word by learning a new Mighty Memory Verse.**

Be sure to mail the envelope and let the kids know next week that the package of peaceful greetings is on its way.

# SUPER SCRIPTURE

Before class, write Matthew 5:9 on a piece of newsprint as in the margin diagram. Underline the words "Blessed" and "sons of God" in red ink and circle the word "peacemakers" in yellow. Be sure to draw arrows from "peacemakers" to "Blessed" and to "sons of God." Tape the newsprint to the wall or door. You may also wish to write the words to the song from this activity on newsprint and tape it to the wall for kids to read as they sing. Copy the Scripture strip for Matthew 5:9 (page 127) for kids to take home.

Read the verse aloud two times, then have kids repeat the verse three times aloud. You may wish to have younger kids echo back the verse in two parts. Then say: **This is a very powerful verse, and it is one that Jesus himself spoke to the people he was teaching. Jesus said that if we're peacemakers, we'll be blessed by God and be called his sons or his children. I've circled the word "peacemakers" in yellow to symbolize the color of peace. I've also underlined what peacemakers will be in the color red. As peacemakers, we'll be both blessed and called children of God. Wow! Just think of how much God wants us to be peacemakers!**

Repeat the verse three more times aloud, then lead kids in the following action song to the tune of the alphabet song.

*BLESSED ARE THE PEACEMAKERS*
*Blessed are the peacemakers,*
*For they'll be called the sons of God.*
*Clap 'n snap 'n turn 'n hop—*
*Bringing peace, they'll never stop.*
*Blessed are the peacemakers,*
*For they'll be called the sons of God.*

After singing, say: **God loves peacemakers. And he loves all people who bring him glory and honor. We may think that God only loves some of us, but God loves all people who love and serve him! We can demonstrate our love for God by bringing peace to other people—**

**even those people who seem different than we are.** Read aloud Romans 10:12, 13 once more, then say: **I'm so glad God made each of us different but loves us all the same! Let's offer a prayer thanking God for his impartial love and for helping us accept others and bring them peace.**

Keep the newsprint with the verse to use next week.

## A POWERFUL PROMISE

Have kids sit in a circle and ask for a moment of silence, then say: **We've learned today that God made us all and that he loves us without playing favorites. We've discovered that even though people are all different, we're to look at their hearts as God does and accept them with love, joy, and peace. And we've started learning a new Mighty Memory Verse that teaches us we're blessed and called children of God when we're peacemakers. Matthew 5:9 says** (pause and encourage kids to repeat the verse with you), **"Blessed are the peacemakers, for they will be called sons of God."**

Hold up the Bible and say: **God wants us to spread peace to all people by respecting them, by accepting them without judging them, and by being kind and considerate. If we do these things, we'll live in peace with people. Let's pass the Bible around our circle. When it's your turn to hold the Bible, say, "Lord, help me accept and respect others and bring your peace to them."** Pass the Bible until everyone has had a turn to hold the Bible. Close with a prayer thanking God for making us all unique and asking for God's help in celebrating the differences in all his people. End with a corporate "amen."

Before kids leave, end with this responsive good-bye:

Leader: **May Christ's peace be with you.**

Children: **And also with you!**

Distribute the Power Page! take-home papers as kids are leaving. Remind kids to take their Scripture strips home to work on during the week. Encourage kids to enjoy the differences in people as they keep peace this week.

# POWER PAGE!

## Peace for Who?

Read the following verses and fill in the missing words. Then write below the word all the answers have in common.

**Acts 2:39:** The promise is for you and your children and for __ __ __  __ __ __ are far off.

**Psalm 67:2:** That your ways may be known on earth, your salvation among __ __ __

__ __ __ __ __ __ __ __.

**Luke 2:10:** I bring you good news of great joy that will be __ __ __ __  __ __ __ people.

**Matthew 24:14:** This gospel of the kingdom will be preached in the whold world as a testimony __ __  __ __ __ nations.

### God shows no favoritism! He wants us ____ to live in peace!

### AROUND THE ROOM!

*Make your own cool "wallpaper" trim strips! Cut pictures of all types of people from magazines, old greeting cards, or newspapers. Glue the pictures to 3-inch-wide, solid-colored ribbon, then staple or pin the ribbon strips close to your ceiling—or use the strips to decorate bookshelves, toy boxes, or mirror edges.*

## LETTER BEFORE

Write the letter that comes <u>before</u> the letter under each space to complete the Mighty Memory Verse.

__ __ __ __ __ __ __  __ __ __  __ __ __  __ __ __ __ __ __ __ __ __ ,
 C M F T T F E  B S F  U I F  Q F B D F N B L F S T

__ __ __  __ __ __ __ __  __ __ __ __  __ __  __ __ __ __ __ __  __ __ __ __
 G P S  U I F Z  X J M M  C F  D B M M F E  T P O T

__ __  __ __ __ .    __ __ __ __ __ __ __ 5:9
 P G  H P E       N B U U I F X

# LIVING IN WORLD PEACE

We can actively bring peace throughout the world.

1 Kings 22:44
2 Chronicles 14:1, 5, 6
2 Corinthians 13:11
1 Thessalonians 5:13
Hebrews 12:14

## SESSION SUPPLIES

★ Bibles

★ a clear bowl of water

★ two pebbles or small stones

★ postcards & yarn

★ clear plastic vinyl paper

★ large manila envelope

★ white paper & index cards

★ fine-tipped permanent black markers

★ colored markers

★ photocopies of Matthew 5:9 (page 127)

★ photocopies of the Power Page! (page 79)

## MIGHTY MEMORY VERSE

Blessed are the peacemakers, for they will be called sons of God. Matthew 5:9

*(For older kids who need an extra challenge, add in Romans 10:13: "Everyone who calls on the name of the Lord will be saved.")*

## SESSION OBJECTIVES

During this session, children will

★ realize they can make a difference in the world

★ understand that God wants all people to be saved

★ recognize the difference between being *at* peace and living *in* peace

★ pray for other countries

## BIBLE BACKGROUND

Would you rather be *at* a car lot or *in* a new car? Would it be more fun to be *at* a pool or *in* the cool water? Most of us would probably choose the "ins," and it's no different with peace. What a wonderful thing it is to be at peace with another country where wars and fighting are a thing of the past. But just think how even more powerful it is to be *living in peace!* Living in peace means to be immersed in peace from the inside out. From serene hearts and peaceful spirits to living in harmony with those around us, living *in* peace is the lifestyle God desires us to have.

Kids know what it's like to be friends with someone one day and find themselves in the midst of squabbles with that same person the next. Peace often seems like a temporary situation to kids—and it often is when they're merely *at* peace with someone or something. It's important for kids to realize that living *in* peace means living with an attitude of peace that transcends situations and becomes second nature to us. Use this lesson to help kids realize they can make a difference in helping others in the world live *in* peace with one another.

## POWER FOCUS

Before class, place a bowl of water on a table and set two pebbles or small stones on the table.

pebble is at the bowl

Warmly greet kids and have them slide on their MP arm bands. Remind them that they're Mentors of Peace who are to carry God's peace into the world. Gather kids around the bowl of water and hand the two pebbles or stones to two volunteers. Say: **I'll give you directions, and let's see if you can place the stones following my words. The rest of us will decide whether you've placed the stones correctly. Give the following directions:**

pebble is in the bowl

★ For the first stone: **Place the stone at the bowl.**

★ For the second stone: **Place the stone in the bowl.**

Have kids decide if the directions were followed. The first stone should be sitting beside the bowl, and the second stone should be in the bowl of water. Then ask:

★ **Is there a difference as to where the stones are? Explain.**

★ **Which stone is completely immersed and covered with water? Which is just beside or next to the water?**

★ **How is being "at" peace different from living "in" peace?**

Say: **We can pretend that this bowl of water represents "peace." When we're *at* peace, we're beside it and next to it but probably not totally committed to peace. It's a situation that could change and may not last. But when we're living *in* peace** (hold up the dripping stone)**, we're** immersed and covered by it! Living in peace becomes our lifestyle as we try to keep peace every day. In other words, peace becomes more than just a situation—it becomes our way of life!

The Bible uses both the phrases "at peace" and "in peace." God's Word teaches that we can be "at peace" with others and that we can also live "in peace." Today we'll discover the differences of being at peace and living in peace with others and why God wants us to do both. We'll explore how we can help carry peace to other countries, and we'll continue learning our Mighty Memory Verse. Right now, let's set these stones aside and explore more about being at peace and living in peace with others around the world.

## THE **MIGHTY** MESSAGE

**POWER POINTERS**

Remind other teachers that your kids are ready and willing to put their peacemaking skills to use! Encourage teachers to call the Mentors of Peace (MPs) when classroom arguments arise.

Before class, use yarn to make a 6-foot circle on the floor. (Tape the yarn in place if needed.) Then write the following verses on index cards:

★ *"Be of one mind, live in peace." 2 Corinthians 13:11*
★ *"Live in peace with each other." 1 Thessalonians 5:13*
★ *"Make every effort to live in peace with all men." Hebrews 12:14*
★ *"The kingdom was at peace under him.... No one was at war with him." 2 Chronicles 14:5, 6*
★ *"Jehoshaphat was also at peace with the king of Israel." 1 Kings 22:44*
★ *"The country was at peace for ten years." 2 Chronicles 14:1*

Have kids stand around the circle and number off by fours. Place an index card with a verse written on it in the center of the circle.

Then say: **I have some Scripture verses about peace. Some of the verses say "at peace," and some say "in peace." I'll place a verse card in the center of the floor and call out a number from one to four. If I call out your number, you must hop to try and be the first to get the card. The person reaching the card first can read it aloud. If the verse talks about being "at peace," the other hoppers must stand at or beside the circle. If** the card talks about being "in peace," the other hoppers can stay where they are inside the circle.

After all of the Scripture verses are read aloud, have kids give each other peaceful high fives. Then say: **In the verses that teach or tell us about being *at* peace with others, it is usually talking about kings or kingdoms. In other words, countries can be at peace with one another—sometimes for years! God wants us to be at peace with other countries and people. But God also wants us to live *in* peace with others. When we have peace in our hearts and are led by God's Spirit, we live in peace. When we trust our country's leaders not to make fights with other lands, we're at peace. Both are good. Both are what God desires.** Ask:

★ **Why is it good to be *at* peace with other countries in the world?**

★ **What things can we do to be *at* peace with others?**

★ **Why is it important to live *in* peace with our families and friends?**

★ **Which is easier: being at peace with the world or living in peace with family and friends? Explain.**

Say: **Sometimes it feels as though there's nothing we can do to make a difference in helping the world be at peace, but there *are* things we can do! We can communicate with others in different countries and learn about their way of life, we can pray for our world leaders, and we can also pray for peace among the people who live around the world. We can serve other countries by sending money to help feed them and Bibles to bring the good news of Jesus to them. And we can also ask God to help us have peaceful spirits so we're living *in* peace while we seek to help the world be *at* peace. Let's make a difference in helping the world be at peace by sending more of our Peacemaker Postcards to a foreign country.**

## THE MESSAGE IN MOTION

Before class, decide if you're purchasing or preparing your postcards and where you'll be sending your cards. (Suggestions for where to send the cards are given later in this activity.) If you're making your own cards, use stiff cardstock or even poster board as postcards. Cut the cards in 3-by-5-inch rectangles and provide markers, paints, or crayons to decorate the cards. You'll need a large envelope and your church's address labels or return-address stamper for the cards.

Have kids work in pairs or trios and hand each person a postcard or blank card. On one side of the cards, have kids write 2 Corinthians 13:11: "Be of one mind, live in peace" (or glue on a photocopy of a Scripture strip of Matthew 5:9). Then have kids add any other message about peace, loving Jesus, or praising God they'd like to tell others. As kids work, tell them where your Peacemaker Postcards will be sent and remind them how reaching out to others with Jesus' love brings peace around the world and gives people a chance to learn about Jesus.

Place a return-address label and stamp on each card. Then slide the cards in a large envelope to mail to a foreign missionary your church sponsors or to an affiliated church in your area. If you prefer, send the cards to Mu Kappa International (MK, a ministry of Barnabas International, establishes missionaries' schools):

Mu Kappa International
P.O. Box 11211
Rockford, IL 61126

When the Peacemaker Postcards are finished, lead kids in singing the P-E-A-C-E Song (page 39). Then say: **Your Peacemaker Postcards are wonderful and an active way to carry the message of peace around the world. One person bringing peace can help and does make a difference. It's been said that the best way to have love is to offer love. In the same way, the best way to have peace is to offer peace. As God's peacemakers, we can bring peace around the world! Now let's see how well you remember our Mighty Memory Verse about being God's peacemakers.**

## SUPER SCRIPTURE

Make sure you have the newsprint from last week with Matthew 5:9 on it. Tape the verse where kids can see. Cut clear vinyl into 8-inch circles and have sheets of white copy paper and markers available. Finally, make a photocopy of the Scripture strip for Matthew 5:9 for each child (page 127).

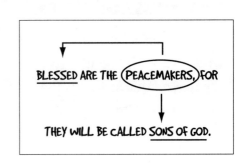

BLESSED ARE THE (PEACEMAKERS,) FOR
THEY WILL BE CALLED SONS OF GOD.

Repeat the verse two times aloud, then challenge pairs of kids to repeat the verse. Have one partner say the first portion of the verse ("Blessed are the peacemakers") and the other partner the last portion of the verse ("for they will be called sons of God"). (If you have older kids, introduce the extra-challenge verse at this time.) Finally, lead kids in singing "Blessed Are the Peacemakers" (page 69). Then ask:

★ **What will we be if we are God's peacemakers?** (point to the words underlined in red ink)

★ **What kinds of blessings will God give us as his peacemakers?**

★ **What are ways we can be peacemakers at home? with friends? around the world?**

Say: **God has promised us that if we're peacemakers, he will bless us and we'll be called his children. That's very special, isn't it? We can make colorful window posters to remind us of the words to our Mighty Memory Verse and also how blessed we are as peacemaking children of God!**

Hand each child a circle of clear plastic vinyl and a Scripture strip. Slide a sheet of white paper under each clear circle (kids can see their work this way). Have kids use fine-tipped permanent black markers to copy Matthew 5:9 from their Scripture strips onto the circles. Then add colorful shapes around the edges of the circles using the water-based colored markers. Outline the shapes using black permanent markers to create a stained-glass look.

As kids work, discuss the blessings that come from being God's children. For example, he hears and answers our prayers, we can trust him to keep his promises, and we enjoy the blessings of a peaceful family.

Tell kids to stick their window posters to their bedroom windows and challenge them to read the verse each morning as they get ready for a peaceful day. Suggest that kids use the Scripture strips as bookmarks. Say: **Let's close our time together by seeing how prayer can help bring peace to the world.**

Keep the newsprint with the verse to use next week.

# A **POWERFUL** PROMISE

Before class, write the names of different countries on index cards (or glue portions of old atlas pages to the cards). Prepare a card for each child.

Gather kids in a circle and say: **We've been learning today that we can make a difference in bringing peace around the world. We've explored the difference of being *at* peace and living *in* peace and how God desires us to do both. And we've reviewed the Mighty Memory Verse that teaches us what we'll be as peacemakers. Matthew 5:9 says** (pause and encourage kids to repeat the verse with you), **"Blessed are the peacemakers, for they will be called sons of God."**

Hand each child an index card and have kids silently read the names of the countries on the cards. Then say: **We can help bring God's peace to the world by praying for countries and world leaders. Let's take turns going around the circle and asking God to help us pray for others. When it's your turn, say, "Lord, help me pray for peace for the country of. . ." and fill in the country on your card. In this way, we can promise to pray for peace all around the world!**

When everyone has had a turn to ask for God's help in praying for the countries, end with a corporate "amen."

End with this responsive good-bye:

Leader: **May God's peace be with you as you pray for world peace.**

Children: **And also with you!**

Distribute the Power Page! take-home papers as kids are leaving. Thank children for coming and encourage them to pray for their countries every day this week. Remind kids to take home their window posters. Keep the MP arm bands to wear next week.

# POWER PAGE!

## → AT or IN ↰

**Read the verses and draw lines to show whether the verse talks about being *at* peace or living *in* peace.**

*1 Kings 22:44*          in
*2 Chron. 14:1*          at
*1 Thess. 5:13*          at
*2 Chron. 14:5, 6*       in
*Hebrews 12:14*          in
*1 Cor. 7:15b*           at

**Now use the code below to discover *why* we're to live *in* peace!**

✜ ☆ ❂ ✔ ◉ ✛ ✦ ✳ ❋
L  C  I  A  E  V  N  D  P

God has __ __ __ __ __ __ __ us to
           ☆  ✔  ✜  ✜  ◉  ❋

__ __ __ __ __ __ __ __ __ __ .
✜ ❂ ✛ ◉   ❂ ✦   ❋ ◉ ✔ ☆ ❂

## Map It out!

Ephesians 1:18 tells us about praying for others, that they may know the Lord. You can pray for others and ask God's peace for them. Attach a world map or atlas page to your wall, door, or bulletin board. Cut out 10 construction-paper hearts and glue them to the ends of push pins. Choose a place to pray for, then mark the place with a heart. Can you pray your way around the world?

## ALPHA-STRINGS

Draw lines from the letters to the spaces, then write the letters in the blanks.

T E E H Y | S B L S E P D C E M A A E K | A S R E L E

B __ __ __ __ __ __  are the  __ __ __ __ __ __ __ __ __ __ __ ,

for __ __ __ __ __  will be  __ __ __ __ __ __ __  __ __ __ __  of

__ __ __ .  Matthew 5:9

S O G O S D N C A L D

Lesson 9

# SHARE A "PEACE" OF LOVE

## Peace is a gift we share with others.

Psalm 29:11
Isaiah 9:6
Micah 5:4, 5
John 14:27

## SESSION SUPPLIES

★ Bibles
★ prepared sugar-cookie dough
★ chocolate & butterscotch chips
★ chopped maraschino cherries
★ shredded coconut
★ plastic bowls & spoons
★ a knife or pizza cutter
★ paper plates or napkins
★ self-adhesive bow
★ postcards or stiff paper
★ markers & church address labels
★ a large manila envelope
★ photocopies of the Whiz Quiz (page 88) and the Power Page! (page 87)

## MIGHTY MEMORY VERSE

Blessed are the peacemakers, for they will be called sons of God. Matthew 5:9
*(For older kids who need an extra challenge, add in Romans 10:13: "Everyone who calls on the name of the Lord will be saved.")*

## SESSION OBJECTIVES

During this session, children will
★ understand God promised us peace
★ realize that peace is a gift
★ learn that the Holy Spirit helps us share the gift of peace
★ thank the Lord for his gift of peace

## BIBLE BACKGROUND

You know the domino effect. Set up the dominoes, tip the first one, and one by one they topple as you enact the chain reaction that eventually, if the dominoes are stacked correctly, reaches every last one of the group. Sharing God's peace is meant to be a chain reaction too. God shared his peace and love by sending his Son to be our Prince of Peace. Jesus willingly shared his peace with us when we said, "Peace I leave with you; my peace I give you" (John 14:27). And now we can share the gift of peace with others in our own families, right next door, or around the world. Peace from God, to Jesus, to us, to others is the

80

chain reaction God wants accomplished so everyone can know and embrace the peace that passes all earthly understanding!

Kids love being able to pass on good things and to share delights with others. And sharing God's great gift of peace can be as fun as it is fulfilling when we prepare to share, then offer the joy we find in peace with others. Use this lesson to help kids understand that peace is a gift God promised, delivered, and shared with the entire world—and now we can too!

# POWER FOCUS

Before class, prepare a cookie-dough "pizza" crust by spreading prepared sugar-cookie dough in a greased pizza pan or on a cookie sheet and baking it according to the package directions. Cool the crust and bring it to class with the edible toppings in plastic bowls. Set the ingredients and cookie pizza on a table. Place plastic spoons in the bowls of toppings, then set the paper plates or napkins beside the bowls.

Warmly greet kids and have them slide on their MP arm bands. Remind kids that they're Mentors of Peace and are to carry God's peace into the world.

Gather kids around the table and say: **Let's share in preparing a special treat to eat later in our lesson. You can share in the preparation by spooning a topping of your choice on top of the pizza.** Let kids take turns adding the toppings of their choice and sprinkling them over the top of the cookie pizza. When the pizza is complete and all the toppings that kids care to add have been added, say:

**Wow! This treat looks good enough to eat, doesn't it? And we'll share our treat in a little while. You all did a great job preparing our pizza.** Ask:

- ★ **How did we prepare our treat?**
- ★ **How do we prepare to share God's peace with others?**
- ★ **Why is sharing the gift of peace with others important?**

Say: **We've learned in previous weeks that peace comes from God. We can think of peace as a perfect gift that the Lord gives us. And peace is a gift that God wants us to share with others. But before we can share peace, we must do a little preparation—just as we prepared our treat before enjoying it. We prepare to share peace by learning about God and his Word, by reading the Bible and obeying the Lord, and through prayer. Today we'll discover more about the gift of peace and how to share this special gift with others. We'll also share our treat and see how sweet sharing something special can be. And we'll review our Mighty Memory Verse that teaches us about being peacemakers.**

**Let's set our Peace Pizza aside for a moment as we explore what it means to share the gift of peace and how Jesus shared with us!**

## POWER POINTERS

*Share peace even further by sharing the Peace Pizza from the Power Focus with another class. Kids will love sharing a piece of peace!*

## THE **MIGHTY** MESSAGE

Have kids stand in a circle. Hold the self-adhesive bow and say: **I have a bow that represents a gift. I'll toss the bow to someone and call out the first letter in the word *peace*. Then we'll keep tossing the bow as we spell p-e-a-c-e. The person who catches the bow after the final "e" will hold the bow as I read a verse. Then we'll answer a question before tossing the bow and spelling the word *peace* again. Ready?**

Toss the bow to a child and say "p." Continue until the word *peace* has been spelled, then read aloud Psalm 29:11. Ask:

★ **Who gives us strength and peace? Why does God give us these things?**

Continue tossing the bow and spelling "peace" again. Then read aloud Isaiah 9:6 and ask:

★ **Who did God share as a gift to the world—who would become our Prince of Peace?**

Spell again, then read aloud Micah 5:4, 5. Ask:

★ **Who did God promise would be our peace and shepherd us as his sheep?**

Spell the word *peace* once more, then read aloud John 14:27. Ask:

★ **What gift did Jesus share with us?**

Set the bow down for a moment, then say: **God promised us Jesus as a special gift of peace, love, and strength for the world. God wanted to share his peace with us, so he sent Jesus. Jesus shared his peace with us and brought us peace by offering forgiveness of our sins. Do you see how this wonderful, perfect gift of God's peace has been shared with us? And now God wants us to continue the sharing!** Ask:

★ **In what ways can we share peace with others?**

★ **When we share peace with others, how are we also sharing Jesus' love with them? God's strength?**

Have kids sit in a small circle and place the Peace Pizza in the center. Say: **Let's share a piece of peace right now! We can share our Peace Pizza with each other to remind us how important it is to share peace with others every day. But before we munch and crunch, let's share a prayer.**

Share a prayer thanking the Lord for sharing his peace with us, then cut the cookie pizza and enjoy it.

## THE MESSAGE IN MOTION

Before class, decide if you will purchase inexpensive postcards or have kids make their own. You'll need a postcard for each child. Decide where you'll be sending your cards. (Suggestions for where to send the cards are given later in this activity.)

Have kids form small groups and distribute the postcards. Let kids write *"Seek peace and pursue it"* (Psalm 34:14) on one side of their cards. Then invite kids to add messages of peace and praise to their cards and decorate the borders if they wish. Add a church address label in the corner of each post card. Put stamps on the cards, then place the post cards in a large manila envelope and send it to a missionary your church supports or to another church in your area. If you prefer, send the cards to:

Team Expansion
c/o Paul Daniels
3700 Hopewell Road
Louisville, KY 40299

Say: **God honors us when we reach out to share the gift of his peace. Remember what our Mighty Memory Verse says about being blessed when we're God's peacemakers? Let's review our Mighty Memory Verse now and see how well you've learned, not only what it says, but also what it means.**

## SUPER SCRIPTURE

Before class, make sure you have the newsprint page on which Matthew 5:9 is written. Cut the verse into as many pieces as there are pairs of kids in class. If your class is very large, write the verse on another sheet or two of newsprint and cut the verses apart.

Lead kids in singing "Blessed Are the Peacemakers" to the tune of the alphabet song.

*BLESSED ARE THE PEACEMAKERS*
*Blessed are the peacemakers,*
*For they'll be called the sons of God.*
*Clap 'n snap 'n turn 'n bop—*
*Bringing peace, they'll never stop.*
*Blessed are the peacemakers,*
*For they'll be called the sons of God.*

After singing, have kids form pairs. Hand each pair a puzzle piece. Tell kids that when you say "go," they're to share their puzzle pieces to recon-struct Matthew 5:9 in as little time as they can. Remind kids to share peacefully and kindly!

After the verse has been reassem-bled, invite pairs of kids to repeat the verse—without looking if they can. Encourage partners to help each other as needed. (If you have older kids, review the extra-challenge verse now.) Then have each pair give each other high fives.

Say: **Matthew 5:9 tells us that if we're peacemakers, God will bless us and call us his sons or children. Did you know there's two other verses about being called "sons of God"?** Read aloud Romans 8:14 and Galatians 3:26, 27. Then ask:

★ **Why do we want to be God's children?**

★ **How can accepting Jesus into our lives bring us the gift of peace?**

Say: **When we're baptized in Jesus and accept him into our lives, we also accept his peace and love. Jesus freely gave us his peace, and he wants us freely to share that gift with others. Then we'll be known as children of God. That's pretty awesome! Let's share the gift of prayer as we thank the Lord for sharing his gift of peace with us.**

# A POWERFUL PROMISE

Have kids sit in a circle and ask for a moment of peaceful silence, then say: **We've learned today that peace is a gift from God and that God sent Jesus to be our Prince of Peace. We learned that Jesus shared his peace with us and wants us to share peace with others. And we reviewed the Mighty Memory Verse that teaches us we'll be blessed and called children of God. Matthew 5:9 says** (pause and encourage kids to repeat the verse with you), **"Blessed are the peacemakers, for they will be called sons of God."** (If older kids are learning the extra-challenge verse, repeat it at this time.)

Hold up the Bible and say: **The Bible teaches us that peace is a gift from God. We'll pass the Bible around our circle, and when it's your turn to hold God's Word, you can say, "Lord, please help me share your gift of peace."** Pass the Bible until everyone has had a chance to hold it. Then join hands and offer a prayer thanking God for his gift of peace in Jesus and for Jesus' gift of peace to us. Ask God to show you ways to share his peace with others, then end with a corporate "amen."

Before kids leave, allow five or ten minutes to complete the Whiz Quiz from page 88. If you run out of time, be sure to do this page first thing next week. The Whiz Quiz is an invaluable tool that allows kids, teachers, and parents see what kids have learned in the previous three weeks.

End with this responsive good-bye:

Leader: **May you share God's peace with others.**

Children: **And also you!**

Distribute the Power Page! take-home papers as kids are leaving. Thank children for coming and encourage them to look for ways to share God's peace with others during the week. Send the MP arm bands home with kids or, if you're continuing the Mentors of Peace program, keep the arm bands in class for the remainder of this book.

# POWER PAGE!

## A "Peace" of Good News!

Share Jesus' peace by sharing the good news with others. Here's some of the good news to share!

- ❤ Jesus gives us his h_____. (1 Peter 1:3)
- ❤ Jesus gives us f_____. (Acts 2:38)
- ❤ Jesus brings us f_____ & l_____. (1 Timothy 1:14)
- ❤ Jesus gives us p_____. (John 14:27)

### Now write one thing you can share about Jesus!

_____

_____

### Fill-'em-In

Write the missing words to the
## MIGHTY MEMORY VERSE

in the spaces below, then fill those words in the puzzle.

_____ are the

_____, for _____

will be _____

_____ of _____.

**Matthew 5:9**

---

## PEACE PIZZA

You shared this sweet treat in class. Now share a piece—and Jesus' peace—with your family!

**You'll need:**
- ★ refrigerator cookie dough
- ★ nonstick pizza pan or cookie sheet
- ★ chocolate & butterscotch chips
- ★ chopped maraschino cherries
- ★ shredded coconut

**Directions:**

**(1)** Preheat oven to 350 degrees. **(2)** Spread cookie dough in pan as crust and bake for 20 minutes. **(3)** Sprinkle with toppings and return to the oven for 5 minutes.

*As you share pieces of Peace Pizza, remind family members how Jesus shared his peace with us! Then read aloud Isaiah 9:6 and John 14:27.*

---

# WHIZ QUIZ

**Draw a line to the correct phrase to finish the sentence.**

- God doesn't                     will be saved.
- All who call on God's name      gift to share.
- We can pray for peace           Prince of Peace.
- Peace is a                      for all nations.
- Jesus is called our             play favorites.

## ⊚ Scripture Swirl ⊚

Write the words to the **MIGHTY MEMORY VERSE** around the swirl. Use the words in the box below, if needed.

called
peacemakers
sons
Blessed
God
are
they
will

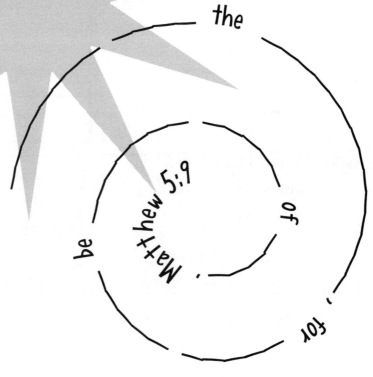

# AT PEACE WITH OURSELVES

The LORD gives strength
to his people;
the LORD blesses his
people with peace.
Psalm 29:11

# INSIDE OUT

Peace in our hearts
is revealed by
our actions.

Proverbs 14:30
Philippians 4:7
Colossians 3:15

## SESSION SUPPLIES

★ Bibles
★ shelf paper
★ construction paper
★ scissors & markers
★ tape or glue
★ newsprint & white paper
★ masking tape
★ rubber bands
★ watercolor paints
★ paintbrushes or cotton
   swabs
★ instrumental music (slow
   and peaceful)
★ photocopies of the Power
   Page! (page 97)

## MIGHTY MEMORY VERSE

The LORD gives strength to his people; the LORD blesses
his people with peace. Psalm 29:11

## SESSION OBJECTIVES

During this session, children will
★ understand that we can trust God's peace
★ learn that having peace helps us live
★ discover that Jesus sought God's peace
★ express a sense of peace in a visual prayer

## BIBLE BACKGROUND

When was the last time you spent fifteen minutes doing
absolutely nothing but listening to your heart, enjoying
peace, serenity, and the refreshment that God gives us
when we take quiet time with him? Chances are, it's been
too long and you'll claim you haven't enough time in your
busy schedule just to be still. But no one was busier and
on more of a vital, life-saving mission than Jesus, and he
knew that seeking time alone with God and taking time out
for heavenly renewal was key in continuing his completion
of God's will. We're told in several places in the Bible that
Jesus went off by himself to be alone and pray—and not
just for a few minutes. Jesus took entire nights to pray and
seek solitude and peace with his Father. If we're to model
Jesus' actions, then surely we have time to seek peace with
God in quiet moments!

Youthful energy and enthusiasm come naturally to kids, and any thoughts of being still or quiet spells b-o-r-i-n-g. But even the liveliest of kids wears down and needs to take time to renew himself or herself. Helping kids discover quiet time with God allows them to experience peace and serenity inside—which can often help outward behavior! Use this lesson to encourage kids to take time to be still before God and feel the perfect peace inside that God gives us when we seek time alone with him.

## POWER focus

Warmly welcome kids and have them form pairs or trios. Have partners lie on the shelf paper and help each other trace their outlines. Tell kids to cut out the figures, then tear or cut construction-paper shapes to make a brain and a heart. Tape or glue the shapes in place on the figures. Don't add facial features yet—you'll do that later in the lesson.

When the figures are complete, have kids "sit" with their paper friends and ask:

★ **How does the way we feel come out in our actions?**

★ **If you're restless and a bit angry, how does it affect the way you treat others?**

★ **How might you act if you're feeling peaceful and happy?**

Say: **We've been spending several weeks learning about peace. We've discovered that peace comes from God, from Jesus, and from being led by the Holy Spirit. We've explored peace with our families, friends, and others around the world. Today we'll begin learning about peace within ourselves and how it helps us live and serve God. And we'll discover a brand new Mighty Memory Verse! Right now, let's use your paper friends to explore how having peace inside of us affects our minds, hearts, and bodies.**

## THE **MIGHTY** MESSAGE

Have kids remain with their partners and hand each child a black or dark-colored marker. Say: **We'll take turns reading verses and deciding which part of the body peace is found in. Then we'll write some peaceful words on our paper friends. Who would like to read the first verse?**

Have a volunteer read aloud Romans 8:6 and tell that when the mind is led by the Holy Spirit, we find peace. Write "Be led by the Spirit" on the top portions of the paper brains or minds. Say: **When we let our brains do all the thinking ourselves and not let God in, things usually become messed up and we end up having troubles and worries! But when our minds are led by the Spirit of God, we find peace!**

Have another volunteer read aloud Isaiah 26:3 and tell that when the mind trusts in God, we find peace. Write the words "Trust God" on the lower portions of the paper brains. Say: **When we trust and obey God, we discover perfect peace!**

Read aloud Colossians 3:15 and Philippians 4:7. Lead kids to see that when our hearts are ruled by Jesus, we'll find peace. Write the words "Christ's peace and love" on the paper hearts. Say: **When we know, love, and follow Jesus, our hearts and minds find peace.**

Read aloud Proverbs 14:30a and have kids tell that peace gives our bodies life. Write the word "life" across the centers of the paper figures. Finally, read aloud Psalm 29:11 and have kids tell that God gives us peace and strength. Write the words "strength" and "peace" down the arms of the paper figures.

### POWER POINTERS

Let kids make "Do Not Disturb—I'm With God!" signs to hang on their doorknobs to signal to others when they're spending quiet time alone with God. Kids love 'em!

Say: **Wow! Your paper people really know where to find peace, don't they? With their help, you can see how peace inside us affects our lives.** Ask:

★ **In what ways does peace help us live? serve God? follow Jesus more closely?**

★ **How is our inner peace tied to our faith in the Lord?**

Say: **When our faith is strong and we trust the Lord, we have peace deep inside us that no one or nothing can take away. Jesus knew about this deep peace and found it when he spent quiet moments alone with God.** Read aloud Luke 5:16 and 6:12, then say: **Jesus knew that we need to be still before God to renew our peace and strength, so he often went away to pray in peace and quiet. Let's discover peace as we silently paint a prayer to God thanking him for our personal, inner peace.**

## THE MESSAGE IN MOTION

Before class, collect watercolor paints, small paintbrushes or cotton swabs, and white paper. Provide quiet, peaceful instrumental music for this activity. Spread tables with newspaper if you desire.

Hand each child a piece of paper and a paintbrush or cotton swab. Quietly read aloud Psalm 46:10, then say: **Let's spend a few still, silent moments with God. Close your eyes and relax and feel the peace the that Lord gives you.** Pause for a few moments, then say: **Now silently think of what you'd like to say to God to thank him for your peaceful heart and mind.** Pause again, then quietly say: **I'll play some soft music as you paint a picture-prayer to God thanking him for the peace he brings. You may express your feelings through a peaceful scene or through soft colors or designs. During our painting time, you cannot talk aloud— just silently in your heart to God. We'll play a few songs, then put our brushes down.**

Begin the music and let kids silently paint what they're feeling. After three or four songs, turn off the music and tell kids to set their brushes down. Join hands and say a corporate "amen." Then say: **Jesus knew how important it is to be still and to spend quiet time with God. Jesus knew that in the stillness, God renews our peace. I challenge you to spend at least five minutes being still with God each day during the coming week** and to experience the peace God gives you as you thank him for his perfect peace.

Jesus found peace in being still with God. He also found peace in his heavenly Father's Word. Let's discover some peace of our own by learning a new Mighty Memory Verse. Your paper figures can help.

## SUPER SCRIPTURE

Before class, write Psalm 29:11 on a sheet of newsprint and tape it to the wall or door for kids to read. (You'll add the underlining and arrows later.) You'll need two rubber bands for each child.

Gather kids by the newsprint and read Psalm 29:11 two times. Say: **What a powerful Mighty Memory Verse this is! It tells what the Lord does for his people—for us. What does the Lord do for us?** Guide kids to tell that the Lord gives strength to his people, then underline the word "strength." Have kids also tell that the Lord blesses his people with peace, then underline the word "peace."

Say: **Do you see the pattern in this super Scripture?** Point out how both portions of the verse say "the Lord," how one portion says "gives" while the other says "blesses," and how both portions say "his people."

> The LORD gives strength to his people;
> the LORD blesses his people with peace.
>
> Psalm 29:11

Have kids write "The Lord gives" above the word "strength" on the arms of their paper figures, and the words "to his people" beside the word "strength." Next, write the words "The Lord blesses his people with" above the word "peace" on the other arms.

Repeat the verse two more times aloud, then say: **Now let's sing "Blessed Are the Peacemakers" that we learned a few weeks ago. Use rubber bands to fasten the feet of your paper figures to your own feet and gently move along with your paper pals as we sing.**

*BLESSED ARE THE PEACEMAKERS*
*Blessed are the peacemakers,*
*For they'll be called the sons of God.*

*Clap 'n snap 'n turn 'n hop—*
*Bringing peace, they'll never stop.*
*Blessed are the peacemakers,*
*For they'll be called the sons of God.*

After singing together, say: **That was fun! I like being God's peace-maker, and I know that it's so much easier to be a peacemaker if I have a sense of peace in my heart. Let's offer God a prayer asking him to help us feel peace inside so we can serve and make peace better on the outside!** Set the paper figures nearby.

## A POWERFUL PROMISE

Gather kids and say: **This has been a peaceful time together, hasn't it? We've learned more about having peace inside and how it affects our lives and the ways in which we serve God. We've discovered that even Jesus took time out to be still and pray to God to renew his peace. And we began learning a new Mighty Memory Verse that says** (pause and encourage kids to repeat the verse with you), **"The Lord gives strength to his people; the Lord blesses his people with peace," Psalm 29:11.**

Hold up the Bible and say: **God's Word tells us to be still and to know that God is God. When we take quiet time alone with God in prayer, he renews our inner peace. We'll pass the Bible, and when it's your turn to hold the Bible, you can say, "Lord, please help me find peace with you."** Pass the Bible and continue until everyone has had a turn to ask for God's help. Then end with a prayer thanking God for the peace he gives us inside our hearts and minds.

Say: **Peace in our hearts feels so good, it makes us smile all over! Let's draw smiles on our paper pals to remind us that God's peace inside comes out on the outside.** Use markers to draw happy faces on the paper figures.

End with this responsive good-bye:

Leader: **May God's peace be in your hearts.**

Children: And also in yours!

Distribute the Power Page! take-home papers as kids are leaving. Thank children for coming and encourage them to spend quiet, peaceful times with God this week. Remind kids to take their paper figures home and to use them to learn the Mighty Memory Verse.

# POWER PAGE!

## Peace Puzzler

Fill in the spaces below. The circled letters spell out another word for peace!

opposite of "go"  ⃝ _ _ _

our Savior  _ ⃝ _ _ _

what God gives us  _ _ ⃝ _ _ _ _ _
(Psalm 29:11)

Jesus left us this  _ _ ⃝ _ _ _
(John 14:27)

opposite of "over"  _ _ ⃝ _ _ _

we're led by God's  _ _ ⃝ _ _ _
(Romans 8:6)

faith's friend  ⃝ _ _ _ _
(Proverbs 3:5)

the color of butter  ⃝ _ _ _ _ _

## PLAN FOR PEACE

*Fill in your own personal Peace Plan, then follow it every day for a week.*

When I can be alone with God, I can

_____

What I can tell God _____

_____

What troubles I can give to God

1. _____

2. _____

3. _____

How I can thank God for his help and

peace _____

_____

## Seek-n-Search

*Draw a line through the words to Psalm 29:11a ("The LORD gives strength to his people") across and down. Then write the extra letters in order on the spaces below to find what we have with God's strength.*

_ _ _ _ _ _ _ _ _ _ _ _ !

| W | P | E | O | P | L | E | E |
|---|---|---|---|---|---|---|---|
| T | O | L | T | H | A | V | E |
| P | E | O | H | H | I | S | A |
| S | T | R | E | N | G | T | H |
| C | E | D | G | I | V | E | S |

# A TIME FOR PEACE

God helps us know
when it's right
to fight.

Deuteronomy 6:18, 19
Ecclesiastes 3:8
Matthew 10:34
1 Timothy 6:12

## SESSION SUPPLIES

★ Bibles
★ cardboard
★ construction paper
★ scissors, markers, & tape
★ 10-inch round plate
★ stapler & brass paper fasteners
★ fine-tipped permanent markers
★ party-favor watches
★ aluminum foil
★ photocopies of the sandal
  pattern (page 126)
★ photocopies of Psalm 29:11
  (page 127)
★ photocopies of the Power
  Page! (page 105)

## MIGHTY MEMORY VERSE

The LORD gives strength to his people; the LORD blesses his people with peace. Psalm 29:11
*(For older kids who need an extra challenge, add in Philippians 4:7: "And the peace of God, which transcends all understanding, will guard your hearts and your minds in Christ Jesus.")*

## SESSION OBJECTIVES

During this session, children will
★ understand that God gives us discernment
★ learn that there are times to stand up and fight
★ realize that Satan tries to steal away our peace
★ know that faith keeps peace in our hearts

## BIBLE BACKGROUND

You've been asked to go along with a lie at work and know the dishonesty will hurt others. But you're a Christian and have been called to peace. What do you do at this crossroads? Take the stance that says, "It's my employer. I should be loyal, and after all, I might lose my job! Guess I'll keep the peace and not rock the boat"? Or do you say, "This is a time to stand firm and be truthful even though I may face ridicule or worse if I can't make peace"? Tough decision ... or is it? God does call us to be peacemakers, but when doing so collides with our faith and God's discernment tells us something is wrong, God calls us to stand firm. Even Jesus knew what Ecclesiastes 3:8 teaches: there's "a time for war and a time for peace."

Kids are just realizing that there is such a thing as telling the difference between what's right and wrong in God's eyes. Discernment is a big word but important for kids to understand and seek. It's also important for kids to know that when their faith in or obedience to God are threatened, they must be courageous and fight the good fight as 1 Timothy 6:12 teaches us. Use this lesson to explore when it's good to make peace and when it's right to stand firm in God's Word and will.

# POWER FOCUS

Before class, collect the craft supplies to make shields, swords, and sandals. For the shields and swords, you'll need cardboard, aluminum foil, brass paper fasteners, and a 10-inch round plate to trace. (Using the margin illustration as a guide, make a sword pattern to trace.) For the sandals, you'll need cardboard, construction paper, and a stapler. You'll also need two enlarged copies of the sandal pattern from page 126 for each child. Place materials for each item in a separate section on the room and place scissors at each craft station.

Welcome kids warmly and let them know you're glad they've come. Gather kids and ask them if there's any good time to stand up and fight for anything or anyone. Have kids explain their answers, then say: **We've spent several weeks exploring peace and what it takes to be God's peace-makers. Today we'll explore the question of when, if ever, God wants us to stand up and fight. We'll look at Jesus' examples and how discernment, or knowing what's right and wrong, helps us decide when to stand firm. But first we need to make three items that will help us learn about fighting the good fight: a shield of faith, a sword of the Spirit, and sandals that are the gospel of peace.**

Form three groups and have each group go to a different station to quickly prepare their items. For a shield, cut cardboard into a 10-inch circle and

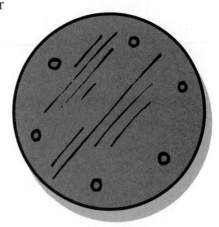

fasten six brass fasteners around the edge. For swords, trace the pattern on cardboard and cut it out. Cover the blade portion with foil. For the sandals, trace the pattern twice on cardboard (or foam) to make a pair of sandal soles. Cut wide construction paper strips to fit over the soles to make sandal "slides."

Staple the strips in place and have kids slide their feet (shoes on or off) into the sandals.

When the items are finished, say: **Let's see, you have the shield of faith, the sword of the Spirit, and the sandals of the gospel of peace. I think we're ready to explore when and if God calls us to stand up and stand firm!**

## POWER POINTERS

Consider making this an even more memorable lesson by purchasing plastic watches for the Message in Motion relay. Check out discount stores or the Oriental Trading Company at 1-800-246-8400.

## THE MIGHTY MESSAGE

Before class, make a sign that says "peace" and one that says "stand firm" and tape them at opposite ends of the room.

Have kids stand in a circle in the center of the room holding their swords and shields and wearing their sandals. Say: **At one end of the room there's a sign that says "peace," and at the opposite end is a sign that says "stand firm," which means fight for what's right. I'll read a Scripture verse. If you think it calls us to show peace, run to the peace sign and lay down your sword and shield. If you think the verse calls us to stand firm, run to that sign and hold your shield and sword in front of you.**

Read aloud the following verses, then ask the accompanying questions before reading the next verse.

★ Deuteronomy 6:18, 19. **How should we respond when God calls us to stand firm? Why?**

★ Psalm 29:11. **How does having God's peace within us strengthen us?**

★ Psalm 20:7, 8. **Why does God fight his enemies and want us to stop Satan from hurting others?**

★ 1 Timothy 6:12a. **How does faith help us have peace? Why is our faith important and precious enough to stand up for?**

★ Proverbs 14:30a. **In what ways does peace help us live day to day?**

★ Ecclesiastes 3:8. **Is there a time to make peace and a time to stand up for our faith and for God? Explain.**

Have kids sit in a circle. Say: **Whew! There's a lot of teaching about both peace and standing firm in the Bible, isn't there? That's because God wants us to be peacemakers whenever we can, but if it means losing our faith or disobeying God, we're to fight the good fight of faith just as God's Word tells us. Listen to how Jesus reacted when Satan tried to steal away his faith in God and when people were treating God with disrespect.** Read aloud Matthew 21:12, 13 and Luke 4:3, 4. Ask:

★ **Why did Jesus become angry when people at the temple were stealing and cheating?**

★ **How did Jesus battle Satan and stand firm?**

★ **How does God's Word helps us stand firm too?**

Say: **God wants us to be peacemakers. But he also lets us know right from wrong and when to stand up for faith and what he tells us is right—and that takes courage! But God gives us the way to fight the good fight of faith! God gives us his Word as the sword of the Spirit, which Jesus used against Satan.** Write "God's Word" on the handles of the swords.

Continue: **God also gives us the shield of faith because faith helps us remain in God. Jesus used this as well.** Write "faith" across the shields. **And God gives us the shoes of the gospel of peace, which helps us be ready to fight the good fight.** Write the words "gospel of peace" on the sandals. Say: **Just as the Bible tells us, there is "a time for war and a time for pcacc," and God helps us know the difference! Now let's take time for a lively relay race as we learn more about God's time for peace and for standing firm.**

## THE MESSAGE IN MOTION

Before class, use cardboard and markers to make two large clock faces (but don't add the hands yet!). Write Ecclesiastes 3:1, "There is a time for everything," on the clock faces, then cut the clocks apart into at least ten pieces. Make two sets of clock hands from cardboard and have ready two paper fasteners. You'll also need a plastic party-favor watch for each child and fine-tipped permanent markers. (See the Power Pointer for even more fun!)

Form two groups at one end of the room and hand each team a roll of tape. Place the two sets of clock pieces at the opposite end of the room. Explain that when you say "go," the first players in each line hop to the pile of pieces, choose one and hop back. As kids bring clock pieces back to their teams, have the teams assemble the clocks using tape, then finish by attaching the clock hands with the paper fasteners.

When both clocks are assembled, say: **You assembled your clocks in record time! Who can read the verse on the clock faces?**

Pause while a volunteer reads the verses, then hand each child a plastic watch and help kids write "Peace" on one side of the watchband and "in God's time!" on the other side. Then ask:

★ **Why is it good that all things happen in God's time?**

★ **Why do you think God calls us to peace? Why does he want us to stand firm when it's time?**

★ **What are ways we can defend our faith peacefully?**

Say: **Jesus once said that he didn't come to make peace—he came to bring a sword. Jesus said this to teach us that some people won't accept him no matter how hard or peaceably we try. Jesus said he brought a sword to teach us that there will be division because he knew Satan would try to steal our faith and the other good things God brings. But Jesus also brought a sword—the sword of the Spirit—to give us God's truths to help us fight the good fight of faith and to be peacemakers when we can! Let's learn a portion of the sword of the Spirit by reviewing our Mighty Memory Verse. You'll need your swords to help.**

## SUPER SCRIPTURE

Before class, be sure you've made a photocopy of the Scripture strip for Psalm 29:11 from page 127 for each child.

Gather kids in a circle and repeat Psalm 29:11 two times aloud. Then have one child step forward to challenge someone in the circle to repeat the verse. The chosen child will step forward with sword held high and repeat the Mighty Memory Verse. If someone needs help, the child who chose the other can help. Continue until everyone has repeated the verse and reference. (If you have older kids, introduce the extra-challenge verse at this time.) Then hand out the Scripture strips and have kids tape the verse to the handles of their swords.

Say: **God gives us his Word as a way to bring peace and also to fight the good fight of faith. Jesus used God's Word to fight Satan in the wilderness, and we can defeat Satan by using God's Word too!**

End by singing "Blessed Are the Peacemakers," or, if your kids know it, the old' favorite "The Lord's Army."

**BLESSED ARE THE PEACEMAKERS**
*Blessed are the peacemakers,*
*For they'll be called the sons of God.*
*Clap 'n snap 'n turn 'n hop—*
*Bringing peace, they'll never stop.*
*Blessed are the peacemakers,*
*For they'll be called the sons of God.*

After singing together, say: **We're called to peace by God, but God also calls us to fight the good fight of faith. And it's wonderful to know that God helps us know when to make peace and when to stand firm and that he gives us the ways to do both! Fighting to ride in the front seat of the car isn't worth the fight and can be settled peacefully. But when Satan tries to steal our faith or peace, God calls us to stand firm! Let's end by sharing a prayer thanking God for giving us discernment in knowing when to be peacemakers and when to stand firm and fight the good fight of faith.**

# A POWERFUL PROMISE

Gather kids in a circle and say: **Today we've discovered that God has a time for everything and that he helps us know when it's time for peace and when it's time to stand firm. We've learned that Jesus stood firm against Satan by using the sword of the Spirit and the shield of faith. And we reviewed Psalm 29:11.** Repeat the Mighty Memory Verse. Then hold up the Bible and say: **Here's our real sword of the Spirit—the Bible. God's Word teaches us when it's a time for peace, when it's a time to stand firm, and how to do both as peacefully as possible. Let's pass the Bible.**

**When it's your turn to hold the sword of the Spirit, say, "Lord, please help me be a courageous peacemaker."**

After everyone has had a turn to hold the Bible, share a prayer thanking God for discernment in knowing when to make peace and when to stand firm and fight the good fight of faith. End with a corporate "amen."

Close with this responsive good-bye:

Leader: **May God's wisdom be with you.**

Children: **And also with you!**

Distribute the Power Page! take-home papers as kids are leaving.

Thank children for coming and encourage them to place their shields, swords, and sandals on the paper figures from last week as reminders of when to make peace and when to stand firm in faith.

# POWER PAGE!

## STAND FIRM FOR PEACE!

Find the missing word in each verse and write it in the spaces. Then fill in the letters at the bottom to discover what there's a time for (Eccles. 3:8).

Psalm 84:11    __ H __ __ __ __
                 4

Psalm 29:11    __ __ R __ __ __ __
            7   9     1

Isaiah 26:3    __ __ __ F __ __
         10 11 6   14 13

Philippians 4:7   G __ __ __
                  5

Psalm 20:8    __ __ R __ __
            2   3

1 Timothy 6:12a __ __ __ T __
           12 8

There's a __ __ __ __ for W __ __ and
       1 2 3 4       5 6

a __ __ __ __ for __ __ __ __ __ .
   7 8 3 9     10 11 12 13 14

## PEACE POCKET

Make a Peace Pocket, then write down the things each day that keep you from feeling peaceful. Slide them in the Peace Pocket and let Jesus give you his peace in exchange!

1. Enlarge the pocket pattern on construction paper.
2. Cut out the pocket and fold back on the dotted line. Tape the sides together, but don't tape the top!
3. Decorate your Peace Pocket with stickers, markers, glitter, or sequins.

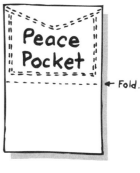

*Follow the arrows to plug in the missing letters from Psalm 29:11*

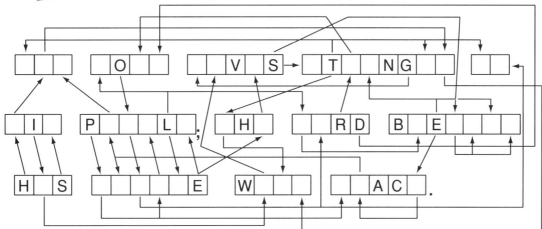

# HONOR IN PEACE

Having a spirit of peace helps us honor God.

Deuteronomy 10:12
Psalm 29:2
John 4:24
Romans 8:14

## SESSION SUPPLIES

★ Bibles
★ paper lunch sacks
★ construction paper
★ scissors & markers
★ tape & glue
★ glitter
★ two small erasers or balls
★ poster board
★ photocopies of the Worship Wreath verses (page 125)
★ photocopies of the Whiz Quiz (page 114) and the Power Page! (page 113)

## MIGHTY MEMORY VERSE

The LORD gives strength to his people; the LORD blesses his people with peace. Psalm 29:11
*(For older kids who need an extra challenge, add in Philippians 4:7: "And the peace of God, which transcends all understanding, will guard your hearts and your minds in Christ Jesus.")*

## SESSION OBJECTIVES

During this session, children will
★ learn what it means to honor God
★ explore how peace and honoring God are connected
★ discover that peace comes from God's truth
★ honor God with prayers of thanks

## BIBLE BACKGROUND

When was the last time you felt worried, anxious, and full of unrest? We all experience these feelings at different times in our lives, and when the "blahs" hit, it's often tough to do the most basic of things. Our jobs suffer, we lose concentration paying bills, we become distracted with our kids, and we feel as if we're bumbling along and not getting anywhere. We want to get away from the anxious unrest and find peace—but therein lies the irony! When we're filled with worry and unrest, it keeps us trapped inside ourselves and makes it impossible to reach out to others or honor and praise God with a whole spirit that in turn gives us peace. But when we take time to remember who our inner peace radiates from, God will establish the peace that finally sets our hearts and minds free to honor him fully!

Worries, anxieties, and unrest aren't a market cornered by adults. Kids suffer from these debilitating feelings every bit as much as the grown-ups around them but find it tougher to release the feelings and find peace. Kids need to understand that having peace in our hearts and minds helps us draw closer to God and honor him, which in turn gives us even more inner serenity. Use this lesson to help kids understand that peace is connected to praise and serenity of spirit to worshiping God.

## POWER FOCUS

Before class, prepare a lunch sack with hidden flaps as follows. (You'll need scissors, tape, and two paper lunch sacks.) Cut the sides from one lunch sack to make flaps. Tape each flap inside a second paper sack along the sides to make "false sides." Tape the flap along the inside bottom and about halfway up the sides. Your goal is to make the inside of the sack look as if no flaps are present!

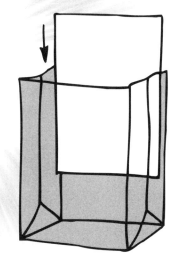

During your activity, you'll be placing papers in one flap while the kids think you're placing them in the body of the sack. The other side will hold a preinserted paper heart that will shake out when you turn the sack upside down, holding the other flap closed. It's a great illusion, but practice it several times to be smooth with your presentation! You'll also need to cut out a construction-paper heart and write "peace through Jesus" on it. Then tear four ragged shapes and write the following words on them: anger, meanness, hate, unrest. Slide the paper heart in one hidden flap and hold it securely closed. Remember which flap has the heart in it! (Hint: Hold both flaps closed until you're ready to insert the ragged papers.)

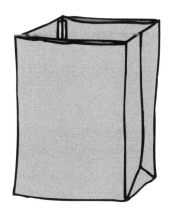

Welcome kids warmly and gather them around the paper sack. Be sure the heart is hidden, the ragged scraps are beside you, and you're holding both flaps tightly closed. Say: **I want to tell you a little about one of the Lord's most peaceful men in the New Testament. His name was Paul, and though he established many churches for Jesus and took the Good News all over the world, he wasn't always such a peaceful man of purpose! Before he was called Paul, he was known as Saul. After Jesus died for our sins and was risen to life again, Saul spent his days persecuting or hurting people who loved and believed in Jesus. Was Paul's heart an empty void?**

Quickly hold the sack open and shake it upside down to show that it's "empty." (Hold on to the flaps!) **Oh, no! Saul's heart had many ugly things in it—things like anger** (drop the ragged paper with the word "anger" on it into the flap that is NOT holding the paper heart), **meanness, hate, and unrest.** (Drop each of these papers into the flap, then hold the flap tightly closed so they don't fall out.)

**Saul had no peace because his heart wasn't ruled by Jesus. But one day, Jesus appeared to Saul on the road to Damascus and changed Saul's life. The change was so big that Saul even started using the name Paul. From that moment on, Paul believed in Jesus and loved him with all his heart. Paul's life had been changed by the peace Jesus brought him, and Paul wanted others to know and love Jesus too. So Paul set up churches all over the world for Christ! Paul spent the rest of his life serving and honoring Jesus. Why?**

Let go of the flap holding the paper heart and let it tumble from the sack without kids seeing the hidden flap. Hold up the heart and say: **Because Paul's heart was ruled by the peace of Christ! Paul had discovered Jesus' peace and all the truth and blessings that come with it. Today, we'll learn more about having peace in our own hearts as we explore how peace and honoring God are connected. Right now, let's make Worship Wreaths as we learn how having peace frees us to love and honor God.**

## POWER POINTERS

Use grapevine wreaths in The Mighty Message. Purchase these inexpensive wreaths at most craft stores or departments, then use tacky craft glue to attach the cards and arrows.

# THE MIGHTY MESSAGE

Before class, photocopy the Worship Wreath verses from page 125, one set for each child. If you're using poster board to make the wreaths (see the Power Pointer for an awesome alternative), cut a 10-inch circle for each child, then cut out the center, leaving a 3-inch-wide wreath edge.

Distribute the paper wreaths and Worship Wreath verse pages. Have kids form small groups and hand each group scissors, glue, and construction paper.

Say: **We'll read the verses on your papers, then answer questions as you attach them to your wreaths. Who can find and read aloud John 4:24?** Have a volunteer read the verse aloud, then say: **God is all truth and is spirit. He's not flesh and blood as we are, but power, spirit, and truth. Let's glue this verse at the top of the wreaths to show this is where we begin peace, truth, and worship.** Pause while kids cut out the verse boxes and glue them to the tops of their wreaths. Then say: **Now cut out a 3-inch triangle. This is an arrow point that we'll use to point the way to the next verse.** Show kids how to glue the arrows to the wreaths (see illustration). Add a bit of glitter to each arrow. Then read aloud Romans 8:14 and remind kids that when we're led by God's Spirit, we are called his children. Glue the verses in place and add another arrow point.

Read aloud Deuteronomy 10:12, then ask:

★ **How does being a child of God's help us obey, love, and serve him?**

★ **In what ways are worshiping and honoring God ways to serve him?**

Glue the verse in place and add a third arrow point. Then read aloud Psalm 29:2. Say: **When we serve God, we can worship and honor him in all his glory and holiness! Honoring God means giving God the glory and the praise for all things. Glue your verse in place, then add one last arrow point.**

When the arrow points are attached, ask:

★ **What verse does our last arrow lead us back to?**

★ **How does having peace in our hearts help us honor God in spirit and in truth?**

Say: **When we know that God is truth and spirit, when we realize that we're led by God's Spirit, when we understand we have peace through the Spirit—then we can honor God in spirit and in truth through the peace in our hearts. What a neat, connected circle that makes! Paul knew all about the connection between peace and honoring the Lord when he traveled to bring Christ's peace to many people. And Paul knew that peace in our hearts is life-changing! Let's play a game to remind us how Paul used Jesus' powerful, life-changing peace as we discover where Paul traveled to honor the Lord.**

## THE MESSAGE IN MOTION

Before this activity, write the following sets of biblical places on construction-paper cards: Ephesus & Antioch; Philippi & Thessalonica; Corinth & Athens; Caesarea & Rome; Berea & Derbe. You'll also need two erasers or small balls to pass.

Have kids form two teams and position the teams in two lines facing each other. Designate one end player from team A as the Passer and choose the player at the opposite end of the other line to be that team's Passer. Hand an eraser or ball to each Passer. Now choose the other end players as the Receivers. (See the game diagram.)

Place a card in the center between the lines. Explain that in this game, items will be passed in a zigzag pattern between the lines until the items reach the Receivers on the ends. When a Receiver is handed the passing item, that team's Passer will rush to pick up the card. Then read the places Paul traveled from the card and score one point for that team. Choose new Passers and Receivers and put another card in the center.

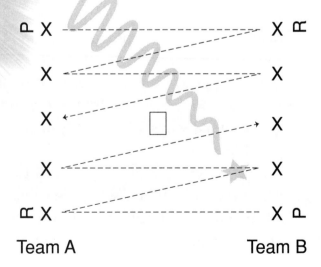

Team A            Team B

Continue playing until all the cards are used. Have the team with the fewest points or cards give high fives to the winning team.

Say: **Look at all the places Paul honored the Lord by spreading Jesus' peace! Paul couldn't have accomplished so much if he hadn't had Christ's peace ruling his own heart. We can learn a great lesson about peace and what it helps us do from Paul. Inner peace from Jesus helps us honor and serve God in wondrous ways! Let's honor God now by reviewing the Mighty Memory Verse.**

## SUPER SCRIPTURE

Repeat the Mighty Memory Verse two times aloud. (If you have older kids, review the extra-challenge verse now.) Then have kids form pairs and challenge partners to repeat Psalm 29:11 as one partner repeats the first portion of the verse and the other partner repeats the second portion. Then ask:

★ **How can we honor God for the blessing he gives us?**

★ **In what ways do being strong in the Lord and having his peace in our hearts help us worship him?**

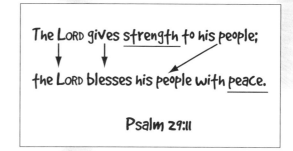

The LORD gives strength to his people;
the LORD blesses his people with peace.

Psalm 29:11

Have kids hold their Worship Wreaths, then say: **Read over the verses on your wreaths—do you see our Mighty Memory Verse anywhere?** Have kids find Psalm 29:11 and read it aloud in unison.

Then say: **The first portion of the verse says that God gives his people strength. But the verse goes on to tell us that God *blesses* his people with peace. Think about the difference between giving something to us and blessing us. God's blessings are wondrous gifts, and when God gives us strength, he blesses us with peace. I think God wants us to know what a gift his peace is and how we can put that gift to use in honoring him and thanking him. Let's offer a prayer of thanks honoring God for giving us strength but blessing us with peace.**

## A POWERFUL PROMISE

Have kids sit in a circle and ask for a moment of silence, then say: **We've learned today that God gives us his peace, strength, and truth and that** we can honor God by giving him glory and praise. We've discovered that having peace inside us helps us honor God, just as Paul discovered when he honored Jesus by establishing churches. And we looked at how God gives us strength yet blesses us with peace. **Psalm 29:11 says** (pause and encourage kids to repeat the verse with you), **"The Lord gives strength to his people; the Lord blesses his people with peace."**

Hold up the Bible and say: **The Bible teaches us that we can honor and worship God in spirit and in truth, and we know that a peaceful heart helps us honor God even more deeply. We'll pass the Bible around the circle. When it's your turn to hold it, you can say, "Lord, I will honor you with peace and praise."** Pass the Bible until everyone has had a turn to hold it, then offer a prayer thanking God for giving us strength and blessing us with peace. Close with a corporate "amen."

Before kids leave, allow five or ten minutes to complete the Whiz Quiz from page 114. If you run out of time, be sure to do this page first thing next week. The Whiz Quiz is an invaluable tool that allows kids, teachers, and parents see what kids have learned in the previous three weeks.

End with this responsive good-bye:

Leader: **May God's peace help you honor him.**

Children: **And also you!**

Distribute the Power Page! take-home papers as kids are leaving and remind kids to take home their Worship Wreaths.

***Have kids take home their Tools of Peace tool-kits***

Thank kids for coming and encourage them to look for ways to honor God in peace this week.

# POWER PAGE!

## PSALM OF PEACE

David knew God's peace—just read Psalm 62, a psalm or poem David wrote about the peace he found in God. Then complete the Psalm of Peace below in your own words!

O Lord, you are mighty and
_____ !
You protect me with your
_____ ,
and give me joy by your
_____ .
Your peace makes me feel
_____ .
Thank you, Lord, for your
_____ .

## Medal of Honor

**Make** this cool chain to wear as you remember to thank and honor God for his perfect peace!

***Whatcha Need:***
★ shiny metal washer
★ neck chain   ★ glitter glue
★ fine-tipped permanent marker

***Whatcha Do:***
**(1)** Clean and shine the metal washer (or paint both sides with metallic model paint). **(2)** Write "HONOR" on one side and "PEACE" on the other. **(3)** Add glitter glue to the edges on both sides. **(4)** Slide the washer on a neck chain.

# SCRIPTURE SCRAMBLER

Unscramble the missing words in the Word Bank and write them in the spaces to complete Psalm 29:11.

The _____ gives _____
to his _____; the Lord _____
his _____ with peace.

## WORD BANK

hgetstrn
drol
sesbles
cepae
epolep
leppeo

# WHIZ QUIZ

**Color in T (true) or F (false) to answer the following questions.**

1. Jesus is the key to our peace.  (T)  (F)

2. A peaceful attitude shows on the outside.  (T)  (F)

3. God doesn't want us to stand firm in our faith.  (T)  (F)

4. Jesus stopped Satan with the sword of the Spirit.  (T)  (F)

5. Paul honored himself by setting up churches.  (T)  (F)

6. Having inner peace helps us honor God.  (T)  (F)

## AIM THE ARROWS

**Draw arrows to place the words in their correct positions to complete the Mighty Memory Verse. The first word has been done for you.**

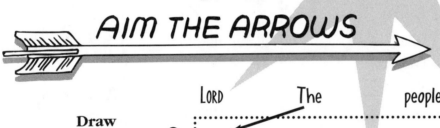

LORD     The     people     gives

LORD    The _____ _____ _____          strength

his    _____ _____ _____ ; _____ _____          his

_____ _____ _____ _____          the

to    _____ _____ _____ , _____ _____ ; _____          Psalm

11

blesses     people     peace     with     29

# REVIEW LESSON

Peacemakers who sow in
peace raise a harvest
of righteousness.
James 3:18

# PEACE MAKERS!

When we're peace-makers, we're kids of the King!

John 14:27
Philippians 4:7
Colossians 3:13, 14

## SESSION SUPPLIES

★ Bibles
★ 10-inch embroidery hoops
★ tacky craft glue
★ clear vinyl
★ stained-glass paints (white, red, green, blue)
★ paintbrushes or cotton swabs
★ olive branch twigs
★ black fine-tipped permanent markers
★ tape & scissors
★ a paper sack gold cord
★ photocopies of the dove pattern (page 126)
★ photocopies of the Scripture strips (page 127)

## MIGHTY MEMORY VERSE

This is a review lesson of all four Mighty Memory Verses: Job 22:21; Colossians 3:15; Matthew 5:9; and Psalm 29:11.

## SESSION OBJECTIVES

During this session, children will
★ realize that peace is life-changing
★ understand that peace draws us nearer to the Lord
★ review peace from God, Jesus, and the Holy Spirit
★ learn that being peacemakers is a lifetime commitment

## BIBLE BACKGROUND

*PEACEMAKER WANTED: Must have wisdom, purity, consideration, submissiveness, sincerity, impartiality, a forgiving spirit, trust, obedience, discernment, and steadfastness. Challenging position but heavenly blessings and full benefits for eternity!*

Sounds like a great position, don't you think? But that list of qualifications! It seems impossibly long and hard to remember. It's a good thing the Bible tells us in Colossians 3:14 that there's one quality that binds all of the above together: love! When we have love and in turn feel love for God, Christ, and the Holy Spirit, we find that being a peacemaker isn't such an impossible job at all, though it's certainly challenging at times. And rewarding? Being God's peacemaker is the most rewarding position you'll ever *live!*

Kids just learning how to be peacemakers are often frustrated that a smile and kind word don't always bring about the peaceful results they were hoping for. After all, there's so much to learn and remember about being God's peacemakers! But kids also need to be understand that the Lord helps them find peaceful solutions to problems with others as powerfully as he gives us peace inside our hearts to carry us through tough days. Use this review lesson to remind kids that the Lord's love is the most powerful peacekeeping tool they need to remember.

## POWER focus

Before class, purchase a large 10-inch plastic or wooden embroidery hoop for each child. Make a copy of the dove pattern from page XX for each child. You'll also need a 12-inch square of clear vinyl for each child (available at fabric or craft stores), an 18-inch length of gold cord, and small Russian olive branch twigs. (If you'd rather, use small silk leafed vines for this activity.) You'll need enough olive twigs or branches for kids to glue leaves around their hoops later in the lesson, plus add small twigs to the beaks of the doves they'll be making. Kids will be making awesome sun-catchers to take home in this review lesson. The cost may be a bit more than most crafts, but you want this lesson to be especially memorable and exciting. For this activity, you'll need just the hoops and clear vinyl.

Welcome kids and ask them if they remember the P-E-A-C-E song (page 39). Lead kids in singing the song and clapping, snapping, or stomping for the missing letters as you sing. When you're finished, **say: That was a rousing start to our time! And this promises to be a rousing lesson to review all we've been learning about peace and being peacemakers. We'll review where our peace comes from and why we're called to be peacemakers. We'll also review the Tools of Peace and how they help us live peacefully with others. Then we'll see how well you remember the Mighty Memory Verses we've learned in the last several weeks so they'll stay fresh and alive in your hearts and minds.**

**As we review all we've been learning, you'll be making super sun-catchers to hang in your windows as reminders of being peacemakers.**

First, you'll need hoops that are as round as the world and remind us we're to be peacemakers with people all over the world. Roll a hoop to each child, then distribute the clear vinyl squares. Show kids how to attach the vinyl in the embroidery hoops, making sure the extra vinyl sticks out the side opposite the flat side. Trim off excess vinyl.

Say: **Now let's review where peace comes from and how having peace helps us live peacefully with others as we honor and serve the Lord.**

## THE MIGHTY MESSAGE

For this activity, you'll need the photocopies of the dove pattern, blue and white stained-glass paints, paintbrushes or cotton swabs, and black fine-tipped permanent markers. (If you have young children and worry about paint smearing, have them use colorful permanent markers instead of the stained-glass paints.)

Have kids stand at one end of the room. Explain that you'll ask review questions from previous lessons. When kids think they know the answer to a question, have them roll their embroidery hoops to the opposite end of the room. Call on a volunteer to answer, then have everyone return to the starting place for the next question. Continue until all the questions have been asked.

★ **Is it possible to have peace if we disobey God? Why or why not?** (No, the Bible tells us there's no peace without obeying God. God is all truth, and wisdom and obeying God brings us peace.)

★ **What does "submitting to God" mean?** (giving up our stubbornness and will; letting God be in control totally.)

★ **How did Jesus bring us peace?** (By dying for the forgiveness of our sins.)

★ **What does it mean to be led by God's Spirit?** (God's Spirit is in control; the Holy Spirit guides and teaches us.)

★ **What are some of the Tools of Peace and how do they help us be peacemakers?** (The tools include forgiveness, love, mercy, kindness, wisdom, and communication.)

**POWER POINTERS**

Photocopy all the Mighty Memory Verses from page 127 on bright neon paper for kids to practice at home in the coming week. Remember: reinforcement means memory!

★ **Why is it important to be at peace within our families?** (God gives us families to love; peace begins at home; when we have peace at home, we can be peaceful outside of home.)

★ **Does God play favorites? Explain.** (No, God loves us all; God made us all special.)

★ **How is being "at" peace different from living "in" peace?** (At peace is a situation and may change; living in peace is an attitude and inside our hearts.)

★ **What does it mean to "fight the good fight of faith"?** (knowing when to stand firm for God and peaceably protect our faith, obedience, and peace.)

★ **How does having peace in our hearts affect our actions and words?** (When we have peace inside us, we speak kind words and serve the Lord and others in love.)

When all the questions have been asked, say: **You did a great job remembering about peace and how peace comes from God, Jesus, and the Holy Spirit. And you remembered that God wants us to be peacemakers with all people whenever we can. Let's add doves to your sun-catchers to remind us how the Bible uses the dove as a symbol of the Holy Spirit and the peace that comes from being led by God's Spirit.**

Have kids tape the patterns upside-down to one side of the clear vinyl so that when the hoops are flipped over, you can read Jesus' name through the vinyl. (You'll remove the paper patterns when kids are finished with the sun-catchers.) Have kids use black fine-tipped permanent markers to trace the patterns onto the vinyl.

Then show kids how to use blue stained-glass paint to paint the name *Jesus* on the vinyl, following the pattern. Use white paint to color in the body of the dove, but not the heart-shaped wings. You'll add the eyes later, after the white paint is dry. When the name and dove have been painted, set the hoops aside.

Say: **Your doves are lovely, and they remind us about being led by the Spirit. And Jesus' name reminds us how he gave us his peace. Now let's play a game as we carry peace to one another!**

## THE MESSAGE IN **MOTION**

Before class, collect Russian olive branches. You'll need two branches for this race and the others for later in the activity.

Have kids form four teams and position two of the lines at one end of the room and the other lines across the room. Hand the two olive branches to the first players in two of the lines. Explain that in this relay, kids will be hopping to present olive branches to the next person in another team's line—not their own lines. As olive branches are presented, kids must say, "Peace I leave with you; my peace I give you." The players who receive the branches then hop to give their branches to someone in another line and so on. Tell kids that they must both present an olive branch and receive one before they can sit in place. Continue until all kids are seated.

When the relay is completed, say: **We learned a few weeks ago that olive branches are symbols of peace. And we also learned that Jesus said, "Peace I leave with you; my peace I give you." Christ has given us his peace to carry to others. Let's add olive branches to your sun-catchers to remind us how important it is to carry Jesus' peace around the world.**

Have kids use green stained-glass paint to carefully add olive branches in the beaks of their doves. If there's time, have kids glue olive leaves around the edges of the embroidery hoops. Then set the sun-catchers aside to dry again.

Say: **Peacemakers know that true peace comes from God and his truth. God gives us his truth in the Bible, which is his Word and the sword of the spirit, as we discovered a week ago. Let's review God's Word now and see how many of our Mighty Memory Verses you remember!**

## **SUPER** SCRIPTURE

Before class, make one or two photocopies of the Scripture strips for all of the Mighty Memory Verses. Cut the strips apart, then cut each strip in half.

You'll need half a Scripture strip for each child, so you may have to use verses more than one time. Place the cut-apart strips in a paper sack.

Have kids sit in a circle, then pass around the sack and have kids each draw out a strip of paper. Tell kids to read their papers but keep them secret. Explain that in this game, one child will begin by reading the first two words in his portion of the verse. Kids who think they have the matching portion of the verse can kneel. The child who read the first two words then calls on someone kneeling and that child can read the first two words from her portion of the verse. If all kids think it's a correct match they can clap. Then both kids read their portions to check and see if the verse truly is a match. If it is, tape the two halves together and place them in the center of the circle. Continue until all the verses have been assembled.

Say: **You did a good job remembering the Mighty Memory Verses. Now let's tell what each verse means!** Allow time for kids to tell what each of the four verses means, then say: **When God's Word is in our hearts and minds, it brings us great peace. Let's add red hearts to our doves to remind us of the peace God's Word brings to our hearts.**

Use red stained-glass paint to add the heart wings to the doves. Caution kids not to smudge or smear the hearts into the white bodies of the doves. Use permanent markers to add the eyes.

When kids finish painting, set aside the sun-catchers, then say: **What fun it is to review all we've learned about peace and being peacemakers. It's good to review to be sure we've learned what God wants us to learn. Let's see ... we need forgiveness and kindness, mercy and obedience, and wisdom and God's Word to find peace. Remember these awesome verses?** Read aloud Colossians 3:13 and 14. Then say: **All of what we need in peace can be tied or bound together with love! Let's end with a loving prayer thanking God, Jesus, and the Holy Spirit for bringing us such perfect love and peace.**

# A POWERFUL PROMISE

Gather kids in a circle and say: **Let's join hands to show how we're all bound in love and peace through God, Jesus, and the Spirit.** After several moments of peaceful silence, pray: **Dear Lord, we thank you for bringing us perfect peace and for showing us how to be your peacemakers. We ask your guidance in knowing how to carry Jesus' peace to our families, our friends, and all across the world. Please help us remember to seek stillness and peace in you when we feel troubled. We love you, Lord. In Jesus' name we pray, amen.**

Say: **Doesn't it feel great to know we're bound in love and peace through the Lord? We can add one last touch to our sun-catchers to remind us of this golden cord!** Help kids tie loops of gold cord through the fasteners on their embroidery hoops.

Lead kids in singing "Blessed Are the Peacemakers" to the tune of the alphabet song.

*BLESSED ARE THE PEACEMAKERS*
*Blessed are the peacemakers,*
*For they'll be called the sons of God.*
*Clap 'n snap 'n turn 'n hop—*
*Bringing peace, they'll never stop.*
*Blessed are the peacemakers,*
*For they'll be called the sons of God.*

Close by reading Philippians 4:7, then end with this responsive good-bye:
Leader: **May perfect peace be with you forever!**
Children: **And also with you!**
Thank children for coming and remind them to take home their Perfect Peace Sun-Catchers to hang in their windows.

# TOOLS OF PEACE

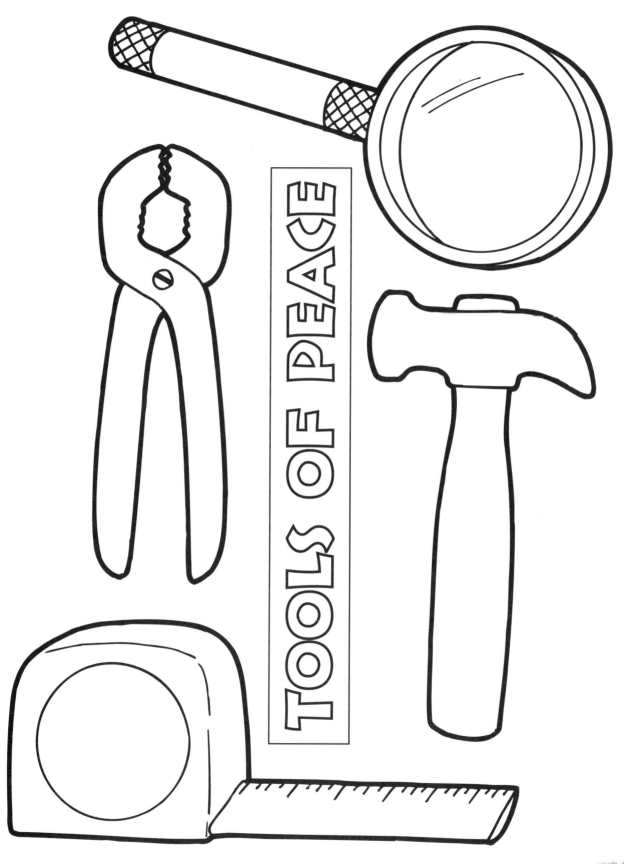

# PAPER PAL PROVERBS

A heart at peace gives life to the body, but envy rots the bones. Proverbs 14:30

When a man's ways are pleasing to the LORD, he makes even his enemies live at peace with him. Proverbs 16:7

A perverse man stirs up dissension, and a gossip separates close friends. Proverbs 16:28

Without wood a fire goes out; without gossip a quarrel dies down. Proverbs 26:20

A friend loves at all times. Proverbs 17:17

He who covers over an offense promotes love, but whoever repeats the matter separates close friends. Proverbs 17:9

A heart at peace gives life to the body, but envy rots the bones. Proverbs 14:30

When a man's ways are pleasing to the LORD, he makes even his enemies live at peace with him. Proverbs 16:7

A perverse man stirs up dissension, and a gossip separates close friends. Proverbs 16:28

Without wood a fire goes out; without gossip a quarrel dies down. Proverbs 26:20

A friend loves at all times. Proverbs 17:17

He who covers over an offense promotes love, but whoever repeats the matter separates close friends. Proverbs 17:9

# WORSHIP WREATH VERSES

God is spirit, and his worshipers must worship in spirit and in truth.
John 4:24

God is spirit, and his worshipers must worship in spirit and in truth.
John 4:24

Those who are led by the Spirit of God are sons of God.
Romans 8:14

Those who are led by the Spirit of God are sons of God.
Romans 8:14

What does the LORD your God ask of you but to fear the LORD your God, to walk in all his ways, to love him, to serve the LORD your God with all your heart and with all your soul.
Deuteronomy 10:12

What does the LORD your God ask of you but to fear the LORD your God, to walk in all his ways, to love him, to serve the LORD your God with all your heart and with all your soul.
Deuteronomy 10:12

Ascribe to the LORD the glory due his name; worship the LORD in the splendor of his holiness.
Psalm 29:2

Ascribe to the LORD the glory due his name; worship the LORD in the splendor of his holiness.
Psalm 29:2

# SANDAL PATTERN

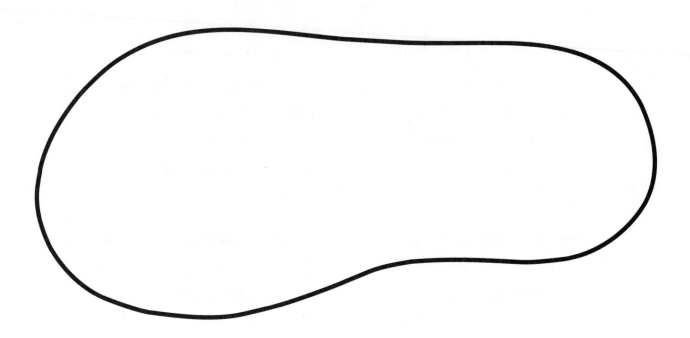

# DOVE PATTERN

# SCRIPTURE STRIPS

Submit to God and be at peace with him; in this way prosperity will come to you. *Job 22:21*

- - - - - - - - - - - - - - - - - - - - - - - - - - - - -

"There is no peace," says the LORD, "for the wicked." *Isaiah 48:22*

Let the peace of Christ rule in your hearts, since as members of one body you were called to peace. And be thankful. *Colossians 3:15*

- - - - - - - - - - - - - - - - - - - - - - - - - - - - -

Peacemakers who sow in peace raise a harvest of righteousness. *James 3:18*

Blessed are the peacemakers, for they will be called sons of God. *Matthew 5:9*

- - - - - - - - - - - - - - - - - - - - - - - - - - - - -

Everyone who calls on the name of the Lord will be saved. *Romans 10:13*

The LORD gives strength to his people; the LORD blesses his people with peace. *Psalm 29:11*

- - - - - - - - - - - - - - - - - - - - - - - - - - - - -

And the peace of God, which transcends all understanding, will guard your hearts and your minds in Christ Jesus. *Philippians 4:7*

# POWER UP YOUR KIDS!

Now there are eight Power Builders books to empower your kids for a lifetime of faith! Susan Lingo's Power Builders curriculum engages kids in learning as much as in fun! Each topical 13-lesson book includes Bible-bound, Scripture-sound, kid-pleasing, life-changing lessons—PLUS teacher training and ways to tell if your kids are really learning. What a powerful combination!

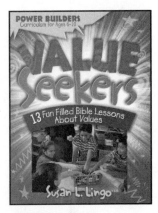

**Value Seekers**
(42111)
Help kids transform their lives by seeking, recognizing, and living by the values Jesus taught.

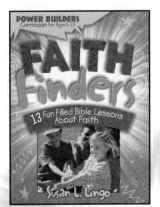

**Faith Finders**
(42112)
Direct kids to discover their own faith in God through Jesus and the Holy Spirit.

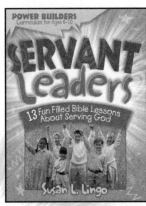

**Servant Leaders**
(42113)
Motivate kids to develop a life-long attitude of serving God and others by examining the lives of Bible times servants.

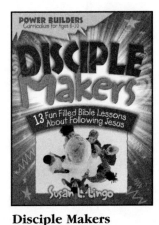

**Disciple Makers**
(42114)
Lead kids to know more about Jesus and equip them to follow Jesus and to disciple others.

**Power Boosters**
(42115)
Empower your kids by helping them discover God's power to change their lives.

**Peace Makers**
(42116)
Build your kids' abilities to be at peace with God, others, and themselves.

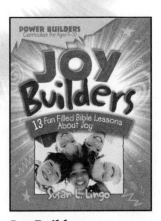

**Joy Builders**
(42117)
Encourage kids to discover the joy of the Lord and to build on that joy by getting to know Jesus more and more.

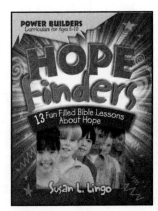

**Hope Finders**
(42118)
Share the hope kids can find in knowing and obeying God and help them live with an eternal hope.

Look for these and other excellent Christian education products by Standard Publishing at your local Christian bookstore or order directly from Standard Publishing by calling 1-800-482-2060.